MW01094038

Advance Praise for *The Healthy Office*

Ninad Tipnis, a valued member of my Abundance360 community since 2016, has crafted an essential guide for the future of work. In *The Healthy Office*, Ninad brilliantly recognizes how mindset and overall health directly impact productivity and success. His innovative concept of workplace "diet" and principles of human-centric design align perfectly with my focus on the intersection of exponential tech like AI and health. Ninad's commitment to creating environments that foster not just productivity but also happiness, fulfillment, and well-being is truly inspiring. I'm proud to support his visionary work in transforming our workspaces into engines of human flourishing.

—Peter Diamandis
Founder of XPRIZE & Abundance 360
Executive Chairman & Co-founder of Singularity
University

The Healthy Office presents a groundbreaking perspective on workspace design. Ninad Tipnis's holistic approach addresses not just the physical layout but also the mental, emotional, and spiritual well-being of team members. This book is an invaluable resource for any organization looking to foster a positive and productive work culture. Ninad's expertise and passion shine through every page, making it an indispensable guide for creating healthy and inspiring workspaces.

—Gino Wickman
Author of *Traction* & *Shine*, Creator of EOS®

The Healthy Office is a testament to Ninad Tipnis' profound understanding of how our surroundings influence our lives and work. I have had the privilege of working with Ninad on the design of our INGOT Brokers office in Amman, and the impact of his work on our team's morale and efficiency has been extraordinary. In this book, Ninad shares his wisdom and practical strategies for creating workspaces that are not only functional but also vibrant and life-enhancing. It's an essential resource for anyone looking to turn their office into a catalyst for growth and well-being.

—Iman Mutlaq
Founder of INGOT Brokers Group

Ninad provides a very practical step-by-step guide for everyone who would like to transform their office but does not quite know how to ignite the process. *The Healthy Office* covers a broad number of design dimensions and emphasizes the importance of the human-centric approach when designing a workspace that not only enhances performance but nourishes the office workers of the future. Definitely a conversation starter in every transformation process.

—Henning Figge
President of Haworth International

This book works wonders on all levels! In *The Healthy Office*, Ninad Tipnis provides a blueprint for creating spaces that nourish the mind, body, and spirit in order to enhance teamwork, well-being, and flow, leading to increased productivity. Each small change can make a difference, and every entrepreneur can benefit from reading it.

—Babs Smith
Co-Founder & CEO of Strategic Coach®

In *The Healthy Office*, Ninad Tipnis delivers a refreshing and important perspective on offices that deliver well-being, vitality, and happiness. With a foundation of human-centricity, he provides pragmatic recommendations for a design that delivers. Ninad's emphasis on the necessity for focus, consistency, and discipline is both real and compelling—and reinforces the need for commitment and attention in order to drive impact. *The Healthy Office* is accessible, insightful, and engaging, making it an essential read for anyone with an interest in the future of work and life.

—Dr. Tracy Brower
Author of *The Secrets to Happiness at Work*
and *Bring Work to Life*

With *The Healthy Office*, Ninad Tipnis has set a new standard for how we should think about our workspaces. His approach goes beyond aesthetics, delving into the profound impact that our environment has on our health and productivity. This book is a powerful tool for anyone aiming to create a workspace that fosters not just efficiency but also joy and well-being. Ninad's expertise and passion for human-centric design shine through every page, making this a must-have for every forward-thinking professional.

—Priti Rathi Gupta
Founder of LXME & Ex-Managing Director of Anand Rathi

In *The Healthy Office*, Ninad Tipnis masterfully bridges the gap between physical well-being and workspace design. Just as athletes need the right nutrition to perform at their best, professionals need a workspace that nurtures their health and creativity. Ninad's insights on integrating holistic wellness into office environments are not only timely but essential for anyone looking to optimize their work-life balance and achieve sustained success.

—Kinita Kadakia-Patel
Founder of MEALpyramid & Author of *The Athlete in You*

The Healthy Office is a groundbreaking guide for the future of workspaces that are vibrant and inviting. Ninad brilliantly shows how your well-being is deeply tied to the environment you work in every day. The concepts are practical yet profound. I've seen the impact of *The Healthy Office* firsthand. Having JTCPL Designs design our office HQ in Southern California, I can personally attest that Ninad and his team are transforming lives for the better!

—Chad Willardson
Founder & President of Pacific Capital and Platinum Elevated, 5x Bestselling Author

As someone who has spent years in the entrepreneurial world, I know the impact that a well-designed workspace can have on creativity, productivity, and overall happiness. Ninad Tipnis' *The Healthy Office* is a masterclass in designing environments that do just that. This book is packed with innovative ideas and practical tips that can help any business leader create a workspace that supports the health and success of their team. Ninad's enthusiasm and knowledge permeate every chapter, offering invaluable insights for those committed to improving their workspace.

—Nick Nanton, Esq.
Emmy Award Winning Director / Producer &
Wall Street Journal Best Selling Author

In *The Healthy Office: Turning Workspaces into Happiness and Success Spaces*, Ninad Tipnis provides a well-researched and practical guide for creating work environments that enhance both productivity and well-being. As someone who has spent decades in engineering and leadership, I appreciate Ninad's methodical approach and the actionable insights he offers. This book is an essential read for anyone looking to integrate wellness into their workspace design.

—Paul D. VanDuyne, PE
President/CEO of IMEG

In *The Healthy Office*, Ninad Tipnis brilliantly reimagines the workplace as a vibrant ecosystem where well-being and success flourish together. With a perfect blend of innovative design principles and deep human insight, Tipnis offers practical strategies to transform sterile spaces into energizing hubs of creativity and health. This book isn't just a guide—it's an inspiring invitation to a more fulfilling work life. A must-read for anyone who believes that our environment shapes our potential, *The Healthy Office* paves the way for a future where workspaces nurture both professional excellence and personal vitality.

—Lior Weinstein
Founder of CTOx – The Fractional Chief Technology Officer Company

As an entrepreneur who understands the value of environment, team retention, and productivity, I can confidently say that *The Healthy Office* is a game-changer. Ninad Tipnis brilliantly combines his architectural expertise with a deep understanding of human well-being, offering practical solutions that any business can implement. This book is a must-read for anyone looking to create a workspace that fosters performance, creativity, and happiness.

—Chris Johnson
Founder & CEO of The Johnson Group

The concept of *The Healthy Office* created by Ninad is revolutionary, to say the least. Imagine transforming our traditional view of workplaces from dull spaces, perhaps with an extra playroom, into sanctuaries of well-being infused with personal goals and relaxed productivity. Ninad approaches these spaces not just from an external perspective but as dynamic, living environments that support the dreams and goals of the organization while catering to the subtle needs of the team involved.

Through *The Healthy Office*, Ninad plants the seed for a new world where workspaces actively enhance human connection, well-being, and the unique aspirations of both organizations and their people. His visionary work redefines what it means to have a truly supportive and effective workspace.

—Dr. Ehab Hamarneh
Transformational teacher, Coach, and Change-leader

Ninad Tipnis's *The Healthy Office* redefines workspace design by integrating health, well-being, and productivity into the core of every environment. Addressing key areas like diet, exercise, sleep, stress, and purpose, Tipnis provides a comprehensive blueprint for creating spaces that truly support and elevate their inhabitants. This aligns perfectly with my "Just Add a Zero™" philosophy, turning inefficiencies into opportunities for exponential success. *The Healthy Office* is a must-read for anyone aiming to design a workspace that inspires, nurtures, and drives modern business success.

—Chad Jenkins
CEO of SeedSpark

As someone who has dedicated his career to fostering a love for sports among the youth, I recognize the profound impact environment has on nurturing potential. Ninad Tipnis' *The Healthy Office* masterfully blends architectural expertise with a deep understanding of well-being, offering transformative insights for creating workspaces that inspire, uplift, and enhance productivity. This book is a must-read for anyone looking to create a vibrant, positive, and successful work environment.

—Vishwas Choksi
Founder of Sports For All (SFA)

Ninad Tipnis's *The Healthy Office* is a game-changer. When JTCPL Designs transformed our Mumbai workspace, our team's creativity and well-being soared. This book captures that magic, offering practical insights that blend innovative design with human-centric thinking. As a leader who's seen the power of a well-designed office, I can't stress enough how valuable this guide is. *The Healthy Office* is your essential blueprint for success, revolutionizing workspaces and unlocking a team's full potential. It's a must-read for anyone committed to creating a thoughtful environment.

—Kailash Biyani
Founder & Managing Director of Asian Market Securities
Private Limited

I can attest to the profound impact of Ninad's design philosophy, having experienced Ninad's work in our Mumbai office. *The Healthy Office* is a masterful blend of insight and practicality, transforming the way we think about workspace design. Ninad has crafted an essential guide for creating productive, healthier, and deeply inspiring work environments. This book is a must-read for any organization looking to elevate their workspace and, in turn, their overall performance.

—Srikanth Velamakanni
Co-founder, Group Chief Executive &
Vice-Chairman, Fractal Analytics

As an investor focused on peak performance, I recognize the crucial impact that environment has on productivity and well-being. *The Healthy Office* by Ninad Tipnis is a groundbreaking guide that reimagines workspace design. Ninad's insights go beyond theory—they offer practical, actionable strategies for creating environments that enhance happiness and success. After experiencing the transformation of our workspace by JTCPL Designs, I can personally attest to the remarkable boost in our team's efficiency and morale. This book is essential reading for anyone looking to elevate their workspace and, in turn, their performance.

—Siddhartha Bhaiya
Managing Director & CIO of Aequitas Investment
Consultancy Private Limited

THE HEALTHY OFFICE

OFFICE

TURNING WORKSPACES INTO HAPPINESS AND SUCCESS SPACES

THE HEALTHY OFFICE

TURNING WORKSPACES INTO HAPPINESS AND SUCCESS SPACES

NINAD TIPNIS

ethos
collective

Printed in the United States of America

Published by Igniting Souls
PO Box 43, Powell, OH 43065
IgnitingSouls.com

LCCN: 2024906423
Paperback ISBN: 978-1-63680-271-8
Hardcover ISBN: 978-1-63680-272-5
e-book ISBN: 978-1-63680-273-2

Available in paperback, hardcover, e-book, and audiobook.

Any Internet addresses (websites, blogs, etc.) and telephone numbers printed in this book are offered as a resource. They are not intended in any way to be or imply an endorsement by Igniting Souls, nor does Igniting Souls vouch for the content of these sites and numbers for the life of this book.

Some names and identifying details may have been changed to protect the privacy of individuals.

Table of Contents

Foreword by Dan Sullivan

It has been my great pleasure working with Ninad Tipnis in Strategic Coach® for the past decade. During this time, I have seen him transform into a leader with a profound vision for workspace design. Ninad's journey is a testament to what can be achieved when passion, dedication, and a relentless pursuit of excellence converge.

From the moment you meet him, you sense Ninad's unique creativity. He sees things differently and puts ideas together in ways that are both innovative and impactful. Despite his calm and soft-spoken demeanor, the power of his ideas is unmistakable. He is not only a visionary but also a thoroughly congenial individual, making him a natural collaborator.

One of the most striking qualities about Ninad is his character. He is a superb human being who exudes integrity and goodness. You get the feeling that everything he touches turns out well because he approaches his work with such genuine care and positive intent.

In *The Healthy Office: Turning Workspaces into Happiness and Success Spaces*, Ninad brings his visionary approach to workspace design. This book reflects his deep understanding of how our environments shape our well-being and productivity. It offers practical strategies for creating spaces that nourish mental, emotional, and physical health, promote collaboration and innovation, and incorporate sustainable practices.

Ninad's dedication to making a positive impact is evident in every page of this book. His insights and practical advice will inspire readers to rethink their workspaces and make meaningful changes. It has been an honor to witness Ninad's journey and see the positive changes he has brought to so many lives.

I am confident that *The Healthy Office* will be an invaluable resource for anyone looking to create a healthier, more productive workspace. Ninad's vision, expertise, and heartfelt approach make this book a must-read for all who aspire to create environments that uplift and inspire.

—Dan Sullivan
Co-founder of Strategic Coach

Preface

My journey into the world of workspace design was as unexpected as it was transformative. A decade into designing various architectural projects, I was far from the realm of interior design. Yet, as fate would have it, my career took a pivotal turn when I was entrusted with designing the retail headquarters for an oil major in India. This project was not just another assignment. It became the cornerstone of my life's work and passion.

The success of this project was a revelation. It ignited an entrepreneurial flame within me, opening my eyes to the relatively unexplored potential in Indian workspace design. This experience led to the birth of JTCPL Designs, a firm that started small but brimmed with eagerness to learn and contribute to this vibrant field. Our mission was clear: to shape Indian workspaces with creativity and purpose.

From the early 2000s to the present, our portfolio has grown to include some of the world's largest corporations across various sectors. Our work has touched numerous industries, from banking, insurance, and asset management companies to IT and Fashion. The diversity of these projects has been an educational journey, constantly refining my understanding and respect for workspace design.

After more than two decades dedicated to workspaces, I sense we are on the brink of a significant shift—a meta-revolution in workspace design. This revolution converges various factors: the evolving needs of knowledge workers, the transition from onsite to hybrid and remote environments, a growing emphasis on health and safety, sustainable practices, and the fascinating advancements in human longevity studies. However, despite the sophistication present in today's workspaces, I noticed a gap in their evolution towards human-centricity.

The Healthy Office **is my endeavour to bridge the principles of human longevity with workspace design, creating environments that are not just functional but also nurturing.**

I firmly believe people are the essence of any enterprise. A thriving workspace places its occupants at its heart. *The Healthy Office* is my endeavour to bridge the principles of human longevity with workspace design, creating environments that are not just functional but also nurturing.

Envision a workplace where every corner, every design choice, fosters a culture of health, innovation, and shared success. A space that is not just about work but about creating a thriving community. This book is a guide to creating such spaces, transforming the ordinary into the extraordinary.

Let's embark on this journey together to discover how every workspace can become a beacon of well-being and productivity. I introduce you to The Healthy Office.

Introduction

If you can imagine an office that is not only a backdrop of your daily tasks but instead forms a canvas for personal and professional vitality, then you are in the right place. Whether you are at the helm, steering the vision of a corporate space, or the heartbeat of the office, ensuring its day-to-day vibrancy, this book is crafted for you.

Gone are the days when offices were mere brick-and-mortar structures housing desks and chairs. Today, a Healthy Office is a vibrant ecosystem where the hum of collaboration, the energy of innovation, and the quiet of concentration coexist. It's a space where natural light replaces the harsh glare of fluorescent bulbs, green plants breathe life into corners, and ergonomic designs support the physical health of its inhabitants. It's an environment that's physically accommodating, mentally stimulating, and emotionally supportive.

My Massively Transformative Purpose (MTP) is to see a billion lives in Healthy Offices. This will not necessarily require a dramatic alteration or a comprehensive overhaul in every office. We have designed offices for nationalities across the globe, and in my twenty-plus years of experience, I have witnessed a tapestry of 'success principles' that echo in every language and culture. These principles don't require major upheaval to uphold, and every one of them supports the most precious resource in any enterprise: People.

An enterprise is an endeavour to improve lives. Somewhere in the mad race of modernity and postmodernity, we have forgotten to prioritise those lives. And no place is more compelled to take care of its people than the office, where people spend more than a third of their lives. I seek to restore nourishing vitality to which every person has a right.

My Massively Transformative Purpose (MTP) is to see a billion lives in Healthy Offices.

In my mind, the office always presents as feminine. Because I perceive the workspace to exude a nurturing, motherly energy, I use "she" and "her" to personify the office. I feel that feminine, caring energy transforms square footage into a living space pulsating with the collective heartbeat of humanity. "Her" corridors echo with stories, "her" walls are painted with ambition, and "her" air is charged with the electric potential of human creativity. In this microcosm of human existence, every individual perspective is a thread woven into the shared fabric of an organisation's purpose. This ecosystem is where humanity is present and celebrated for its very essence.

Our focus in the following chapters is unapologetically human-centric. Each page reveals another aspect of how people in the office can flourish and how their well-being is the bedrock on which towering institutions stand. Drawing upon my years of studies in the science of human longevity, I posit a thrilling hypothesis: What if the secrets of a long, healthy life are inextricably linked to the secrets of vibrant, enduring workspaces?

As you journey through these pages, consider yourself a co-student, learning alongside me. Together, we'll explore how we can infuse our offices with vitality, transforming them into spaces that thrive, not just survive.

While human longevity continues to advance, this book distils the essence of what it means to live well into tangible, achievable actions. We'll discuss interventions that are so simple in concept that they might be overlooked yet are so powerful in practice that they can redefine the health span of an organisation.

Health span, the period of life spent in good health, stands distinct from lifespan. It is not the number of years we count but the quality of life within those years that truly matters. This book is a call to action to extend the health span of each individual within the office environment simply and effectively.

We'll discuss interventions that are so simple in concept that they might be overlooked yet are so powerful in practice that they can redefine the health span of an organisation.

However, a word of caution: simplicity is not synonymous with ease. The path to transforming our offices into havens of health requires Focus, Consistency, and Discipline (FCD). It is not enough to read about these strategies. It is not even enough to agree with them. Democritising the Healthy Office is an actionable commitment that demands daily attention and care.

So, as we embark on this journey together, let's commit to the FCD philosophy. Let's transform not only our workspaces but also the lives of those who inhabit them. Welcome to The Healthy Office.

0.5

The State of the Office

How would you define a proper office space? Maybe you think of minor enhancements to your current office space, such as:

- Updated, comfortable furniture

- Natural lighting

- Reliable air conditioning

- Accessible food and water

- Proximity to home

- Personal space

Now, even if your office had all of these things to the degree of your satisfaction, there is still something missing from this office description. I know plenty of offices that provide all these benefits and more, but people still lack one key component. Happiness!

Any given office can have all the luxuries that money can buy, but the team and their happiness are the true heartbeats of the office. It will always fall short of optimal if they are not at the centre of every consideration.

When people are the focus, walking into your office every day will be like walking into a spa. You can have physical amenities like lighting, comfort, and personal space, but your mental, emotional, spiritual, and physical health will be your priority throughout your workday. For eight hours per day, you will have the perfect conditions to get the most meaningful work done while enjoying yourself in a healthy space.

The Evolution of the Office

Humans have not changed in terms of size and structure for thousands of years. Anatomically, human beings are the same now as they were during the height of ancient civilisations. On the other hand, the human workspace has truly evolved at an astronomical rate. Even if we compare a current workspace with one from fifty or a hundred years ago, we see a significant disparity in physical manifestation. The material, the lighting, the standard of air quality, the furniture, the seating, and, to some degree, even the office function have all changed. We now see more of an emphasis on creative work and thinking within the office rather than the strict adherence to proven processes. Office design reflects this.

The pace of change is vastly different between humans and their work environment. Assuming these trends will continue, the quality and values of office spaces will continue to change and evolve, but humans will remain the same for thousands of years. We cannot achieve a timelessly valuable workspace by concentrating on the design's physical aspects. Physical amenities are lower-level solutions because they are subject to change. Instead, we can focus on ensuring that people thrive in their environment no matter how the physical office attributes might change. In other words, office design must be flexible.

The primary question driving all workspace design must be this: How can the office provide everything necessary for its inhabitants' well-being? What do people need in order to be enlivened by their workspace?

A Healthy Office is a timeless office.

The answer might be a temporary change. It might be a physical aspect that will be obsolete in a hundred years. The strategies for answering this question, however, are evergreen. You will be able to ask the same question and utilise the same strategies in a hundred years because it is a human-centric question. This is the value in taking an office that might be entirely proper and functional now and implementing these timeless strategies for putting people first. A Healthy Office is a timeless office.

The Future of the Office

Although humans are no longer evolving, human longevity is certainly changing. For years, the average lifespan was eighty to ninety years. We pictured an eighty- or ninety-year-old as a weak, frail, dependent human being. With this definition, many people had no desire to extend their lifespan because they didn't want to exist in that frail state any longer than they had to. Recently, we've realised science and technology can extend lifespan and health span along with it. When this happens in the near future, we will see human beings who are vibrant and healthy for much longer.

How does this affect workspaces? The Healthy Office needs to be able to respond to a greater diversity of age groups. On the one hand, health span is lengthening with lifespan. We will not be surprised to see seventy-five-year-olds heading to the office with the same passion and drive as they did at twenty-five.

On the other hand, the value of formal education in the workplace is declining. Employers are looking more for practical experience and less for formal degrees and qualifications. This evolution in the workplace will result in team members as young as fifteen working right alongside seventy-five-year-olds. Both groups will be energetic and committed, contributing fully to the enterprise.

The workspace can only support such a broad range of ages if it employs timeless, human-centric strategies for promoting health. These strategies, when infused into workspace design, will bring people closer. They will provide common points of dialogue. They will tap into the universalities of human experience, transforming workspaces into catalysts for multiple generations to understand themselves and the world around them.

Today, we see an acute disconnect between our generation and those ahead of or behind us. There are few to no common platforms that promote understanding and connectivity. Thanks to The Healthy Office, the workplace can become the common platform where all generations converge. We can only achieve that by letting physical changes and amenities be a low-level solution as they continue to evolve. The higher-level solutions are the incremental methods of protecting and promoting human well-being as the office's primary goal.

In the following chapters, we will explore the facets of a healthy, people-centric office. I will explain why each of these aspects is necessary to The Healthy Office and give you strategies for promoting them in your own office.

W. Clement Stone said that big doors swing on little hinges. Let these small changes be the hinges that swing your office space into a new era of vitality.

Defining The Healthy Office

Attribute	The Status Quo Office	The Healthy Office
Objective	Profit	Happiness
Duration	Temporary	Timeless
Solutions	Low-level physical changes	High-level strategies

So far, the attributes of The Healthy Office include broad changes in perspective. It invariably takes time to make full-fledged shifts in perception, but the first step is to commit to the shift. I invite you now to take a moment and commit to the idea of The Healthy Office.

From now on, the office's purpose is to promote her inhabitants' happiness for as long as possible, using strategies that surpass temporary physical changes.

For a personal introduction to The Healthy Office Movement, follow the QR code below or visit

TheHealthyOffice.Com/Resources

1

Diet

Nourishing Workspaces with Simple Design Solutions

Please allow me to perhaps influence your perception of diet. The word diet comes from the Greek word *diaita*, which means "a way of life." We generally think of diet as a specific system for what you eat and when, but the root of this word implies your diet is about more than just food. Diet refers to your comprehensive way of life, so your health is tied to everything you take in and how you live.

Going deeper, we can identify four types of diets: nutritional, mental, emotional, and spiritual. By exploring each of these areas, we'll identify the different regions of intake in your life and show you how they pertain to your overall health. We'll also reimagine your workspace through the diet lens.

1.1: Nutritional Diet

Fostering Healthy Eating through Workspace Design

We won't spend too much time on nutritional dieting since there's so much information on the topic. It's one of the most well-documented areas of research. A quick Amazon search turns up over 60,000 results for diet-related books. It is a popular topic for good reason. As we know, your diet is your way of life.

Our journey will focus on how nutritional dieting integrates with The Health Office and how workspace design can integrate with your life and move you toward a more productive health span.

Signage

Inspirational signage has been indispensable for many offices wanting to promote healthy living. They might hang up a poster or two of a super healthy rockstar around the office in the hopes of inspiring team members to take control of their lives and make healthy eating choices. While these efforts are no doubt well-intentioned, signage such as this is not motivational for unhealthy people. It can even be intensely depressing. Team members starting their journey toward better health simply do not connect or relate with a poster of a supermodel. It does not reflect an effort to meet people where they are. Instead, it is a snapshot of the end result of a health and diet journey.

Signage in your office can still be helpful, so long as it is educational. You can use environmental graphic design to empower your people with awareness. Whenever change is the goal, education must be the first step. If I am trying to alter the course of my life, however slightly, I must first set out very clearly what I am trying to change, what the individual actions are that will get me there, and above all, why I need to persist with this change.

Likewise, if signage in the office can be informational—gently instructing people in the workplace as to why they might change their diet—then your office can be infinitely more effective in promoting a healthy nutritional diet than the office with the inspirational poster.

This type of signage can instigate change, but a Healthy Office must also maintain change. To this end, consider providing a different kind of signage in designated eating areas, such as digital screens or interactive boards. These might display

- nutritional information
- healthy recipes
- tips for balanced meals

This type of information opens up pathways for people who might not otherwise know how to maintain their nutritional health.

Finally, smart graphics can be useful in upgrading consistent awareness of health. These can be simple messages, like a reminder to hydrate or a recommendation for fruit instead of fruit juice.

You might not consider these to be significant additions to the office, but it is surprising how unaware people can be of good attitudes toward food. Small additions are often the most effective.

Supply

A true Healthy Office can go further than simply informing and inspiring. It can provide the food itself. Some offices offer food for their people. After all, most people spend the majority of their day in the office. Consider installing a nutrition station. Don't overcomplicate the task. It might look similar to a vending machine full of standard snack food and sugar-free drinks. A place that provides healthy options, especially if those food options are varied and appealing, is vital for promoting the health of every person it services.

The first step is to carry out an audit of your office pantry.

Is it full of sweet, salty, processed foods like the typical corporate pantry?

Does your team consume mindless calories through tea and coffee machines?

Are sugary drinks the only option?

What kind of food is being offered to your teammates?

How will these food choices shape your team's way of life?

Forming an accurate analysis of the current conditions may require time, but it is a negligible investment compared to perpetuating unhealthy lifestyles for your colleagues. The next step is to replace everything with locally sourced, fresh, healthy, unprocessed, organic food. The more of these qualities you can achieve for your office pantry, the better.

You might be thinking, "That's great. I would love to see my office provide healthier snacks, but there's nothing I can do about that." To address that concern, let me tell you a story. We helped design an office that took a proactive approach to nutrition. This group of people was dedicated to maintaining a proper diet and lifestyle. They wanted to provide the team with snack options throughout the day, but they knew that a standard vending machine rental would limit their options to sugary candy, potato chips, or other non-nutritional options. Instead of renting, they decided to buy the vending machine. They replaced every typical snack item with wholesome, homemade, substantial food options. This group of people desired healthy standards but also saw their coworkers as the most precious part of their office space and were willing to go to great lengths to ensure a healthy way of life for those around them. Their intervention, however, was simple in the grand scheme of things. Anyone can take a similar step towards promoting intentional food choices.

Take a moment to consider the nutritional situation in your own office. What could you do to foster change? Who else in your proximity wants to see change?

Spaces

Educational signage and healthy food supplies are vital to The Healthy Office, but their effects can be enhanced when paired with a physical space fully dedicated to nutritional diet. When designing, I call these spaces Designated Healthy Eating Zones. Such a zone can take many different forms depending on the size of the office, but there are a few necessary characteristics:

- Food storage facilities

- Comfortable dining spaces

- Areas exclusive to eating

A dining area could be a cafeteria, especially in a larger office, so long as it is designed to be restful and stress-free. Large cafeterias can often have harsh lights and an almost medical feel that is not conducive to a healthy lifestyle. People should be at ease in these spaces.

In smaller offices, a cafe or lounge is adequate for a healthy eating zone. Either way, the space must be conducive to encouraging a healthy diet. It can also promote camaraderie as team members take meals at similar times in cosy spaces.

Another way to increase communal interest in health is to hire a nutritional expert for the workplace. This option may not be feasible for every office, but if possible, it can be an excellent investment. Nutritionists can lead informational events about diet, they can be on call throughout the day to answer questions, and they can make suggestions for healthy snacks and meals. Not only will the team feel cared for, but they will also be healthier and will require less downtime to organise and eat their meals.

1.2: Mental Diet

Enhancing Mental Well-being Through Thoughtful Design

Two people walk into the same office, knowing they each have a long day ahead. This particular space has recently done away with cubicles in an effort to create a better sense of community and camaraderie among team members. For one person—let's call him Adam—this environment energises him, and collaborative conversations help his workday fly by. He returns home at the end of the day in a bright mood, satisfied by all that he was able to accomplish.

The other person, Maya, is not as thrilled about the lack of physical boundaries around her space. The conversations and movements around the space constantly distract her from her task as she greets those around her. She also can't help but feel like her work is a performance because she is visible to the entire workforce, and concentrating on looking right as she works detracts from her productivity. Maya returns home feeling exhausted and thoroughly dissatisfied with her day.

What is the difference between Adam and Maya?

They each have an entirely different mental diet. Neither is bad. They simply respond to the external stimuli of the workplace differently.

Individuals process so much information every day, and in this rapidly progressing world, the amount of information is only increasing. People typically intake eleven million bits of information per second, but they can only consciously process forty bits per second.[1] We must be even more aware of how we personally respond to such stimuli. Everyone has their limits, and knowing those limits protects you from mental fatigue and promotes an optimal quality of life.

One way to know yourself is to identify your personality type.

- Are you an introvert? Are you energised when spending time alone or with a few close friends?

- Are you an extrovert? Do you tend to seek out other people or large groups to recharge?

- Are you an ambivert? Are you extroverted within your tribe but introverted when dealing with many unknown people?

These personality types determine your mental diet and capacity within the workplace. Adam was more energised by the ability to see and engage with people all day long, while

Maya's productivity was inhibited by the inability to retreat from constant social interaction and recharge.

Consider as well that about eighty per cent of the population is neurotypical, while the remaining twenty per cent is neurodivergent. Neurodivergence refers to the discrepancy between personality and brain function.[2] Those with neurodivergent tendencies have entirely unique strengths and needs. As a result, traditional, static office models can limit a person's ability to work authentically and productively.

Not every space in the office has to look the same. People should have the freedom to choose where they are most comfortable.

So, how can workspace design help every personality type flourish in the same office? How can you create external stimuli that will nudge your office occupants toward better functionality?

The short answer: provide variety.

Not every space in the office has to look the same. People should have the freedom to choose where they are most comfortable, but at the same time, they should have the flexibility to move between spaces according to the fluctuations of their mental capacity.

When we design a workspace, we study departmental dynamics and structure the space so that interaction is encouraged because, fundamentally, workspaces need interaction to function. It is also essential to provide a menu of spaces that allow individuals to explore and celebrate their own personalities within the office.

Stefan Kiss, Director of Ideation at Haworth, explains the three ways people use the office, especially in light of the shift to hybrid work. People need space for individual work, collaborative work, and social restorative activities.[3]

The goal of designing an office with a diversity of spaces is to encourage each person to feel their best when in the office. If you know that there is a space designed to celebrate you and your particular personality, then you will feel more motivated to come to the office and prosper there daily.

Of course, it is humanly impossible to map every personality. But what any office designer can do is use personality archetypes. We can map broader personas and design spaces for those. That way, we can find the right space to help each person thrive.

Concentrate

Quiet zones should be the first item on the menu of spaces offered in your office. Whether you call them quiet zones or focus areas, these spaces provide a preparatory strategy for every person in your office. If people have a dedicated quiet space, they can prepare themselves to receive at the right frequency. External factors can be internalised in many different ways. Allowing a space with fewer external stimuli permits people to internalise however necessary.

A focus area is also useful for those who need fewer stimuli in order to be able to concentrate on a single task. For these people, the ability to retreat into a quiet area can be invaluable to their productivity. For others, a short time spent in silence is enough to provide mental rejuvenation for the rest of the workday.

In an existing office, you might decide to designate a particular room to be a quiet area. If you are building or remodelling an office, you could create a soundproofed or otherwise acoustical space where the decibel level is significantly lower than the rest of the office.

Either way, when you designate these spaces, you create loci: identifiable locations that your mind associates with concentration, rejuvenation, or relief from stimuli. As your mind identifies with those places, you are liberated to think expansively and reset your thought processes whenever you need to. These spaces are permanent office fixtures, and even knowing these are available to you can prevent overstimulation.

Julian Treasure, an expert in sound and communication, explains, "We need to give people spaces that match what they need to do." Providing quiet spaces is the first step toward enabling people to do what they need to do.

Collaborate

Sometimes, a quiet space does not match what a person needs to do. Quiet solitude is beneficial, but only to the degree that it enhances the time spent in collaboration with others. Communal areas provide people with the physical capacity to interact effectively and comfortably with their colleagues.

Rather than having an ocean of workstations, desks, or benches, break up the monotony by including open, collaborative spaces. At workstations, conversation is possible, but only with neighbours and at restricting volumes. In a space intended for conversations, occupants are free to talk to anyone. This is not a formal meeting room. It is an informal, spacious area designed for the comfort of open discussion.

When you free your team from the preconceptions that discussions must be formal and work-related, you create an environment conducive to creativity and collaboration. Someone might grab a few coworkers to hash out the details of a project while a few others share weekend stories while on a break. This space is flexible.

Ultimately, a communal space inspires people to vibrate with a positive frequency. Just being around others can create a sense of bonding and cooperative agreement, which is essential to a Healthy Office.

Cultivate

The presence of plants, greenery, or any sort of vegetative life in the office can raise the quality of the environment drastically. We have already seen that external stimuli in the office can either boost or limit productivity based on personality. But any type of beautiful stimulus will almost universally have a positive effect on those influenced by it. As nature is the most innate and constant beauty available to us, we are naturally inclined toward designs inspired by it.

Biophilic design is easy to incorporate. In an existing office, merely garnish your workspace with plants. Invest in landscaping your office internally with houseplants or greenery, or ensure that external landscaping is visible through windows. Often, simply having green in your line of sight as you work can enhance your mood.

If you are remodelling or designing a new office, you can make biophilic elements an essential part of the design. Inset greenery along the walls to create texture and colour, or use tall, leafy plants to provide partial privacy instead of half walls. Whatever you can implement will be a huge step toward creating a grounded and joyful environment.

Biophilic design carries benefits beyond the aesthetic aspects. Living plants create an oxygen-rich atmosphere. Studies show that the introduction of plants into an office setting results in increased concentration and productivity.[4] Some types of plants can significantly improve air quality by removing toxins and chemicals from the environment.[5]

Altogether, biophilic design can substantially benefit the mental and physical health of the office's inhabitants.

Further, plants need light to thrive, and people are no different. Incorporating natural light wherever possible is essential for plant and human health. At JTCPL Designs, we study the sun's path to ensure an office can optimise daylight, which can, too, enhance mood.

Biophilia is still a form of external stimuli. But no matter how you process those stimuli based on your personality type, your mental health will improve with biophilic interventions in the office.

Contemplate

Humans are sensory animals. We have already seen how biophilic elements benefit people while in the workspace, but sometimes interventions don't have to be that complex. Any type of artistic or cultural display will go far to fill that human need for visual satisfaction.

Sculptures are a fantastic investment because they create a point of interest, and they can open a space to break up the visual monotony of the office. But art does not need to be expensive or elaborate. It could be a simple graphic, neatly framed and installed on the wall. The key is for the display to resonate with the whole team, for example:

- A depiction of a historical event with meaning to your company
- The work of local artists
- A project win for your team

- Accomplishments that your team is particularly proud of

- A representation of some vision or goal to inspire your team to press forward

What people see on a daily basis is a significant portion of their mental diet. During the hours spent in the office, you can control part of your mental diet through these interventions. Elevate the quality of your mental diet by using art displays and plants as part of your visual. Create a variety of spaces with varying levels of interaction to ensure that there are restful and healing aspects of your office experience every minute.

> **Emotions prime our minds and bodies for action.**

1.3: Emotional Diet

Supporting Emotional Health through Empathic Design

Emotional diet is tied closely to mental diet, but it has little to do with the external factors of your workspace and everything to do with internal processing. Beatriz Arantes, an environmental psychologist and researcher, explains that emotions link mind and body: "In the simplest sense, work is action—doing something. Emotions prime our minds and bodies for action."[6] If a person cannot easily regulate their emotional state, then any external stimulus can cause a negative internal reaction. That reaction, in turn, causes inefficient, constricted, or even hostile action. The first step to ensuring a balanced or positive emotional diet is acknowledging your current tendencies.

- What is your emotional state?
- What is your exhaustion level?
- How do you handle stress?
- Are your thoughts focused?

No matter how you might answer these or how your answers change from week to week, a Healthy Office can help regulate your emotional diet.

Every strategy that I have seen to be effective for emotional health centres around taking control of your mind and body in manageable ways. When you can reassure yourself of certain constants in your surroundings, it becomes easier to maintain emotional energy and composure. Design strategies can offer a level of control when they allow personalisation rather than standardisation. When people can provide input, they feel seen and trusted. Workspace design, in this case, becomes a catalyst for inner engineering.

Function

To create an environment that promotes emotional regulation, you must first allow individual control over certain addressable parameters. Lighting, for example, can always have manageable variations. Shades or window tint technology can regulate natural light. Artificial light, when necessary, should always be adjustable.

The necessity for regulation applies to air conditioning as well. Although air temperature allows for less individual control, the ability to weigh in on a preferred office temperature helps maintain a sense of power and comfort. At the very least, make individual fans or space heaters available to your office inhabitants so they can make adjustments for their comfort.

Likewise, the use of colour psychology can cater to emotional needs. Cool blues and greens tend to be calming colours, but warm oranges and reds are mentally and emotionally stimulating. Individuals should have the choice to alter the colours of their workspace to support their emotional state. If such personalisation is not possible, a workplace can at least provide a few options inspired by different chromatic feelings. This applies to textures and materials as well. Allowing personal management of sensory stimulation leads to better control over emotional response. It encourages an overall positive emotional environment as well.

These are just a few ways that the functional aspect of the office can create a sense of external control that influences the inner regulation of emotional diet.

Flexibility

We have already seen how different types of spaces can benefit one's mental diet. The ability to choose what space you inhabit can influence your emotional diet as well. If the office has a space intended for socialisation, it grants inhabitants the flexibility to break free of hardcore formal work zones, which might constrict emotional expression. These spaces encourage the spirit of collaboration and invite team members to build mutually supportive relationships.

When someone needs emotional support from others, they always have the opportunity to enter this communal space to seek out support without announcing it. Alternatively, if someone needs isolation in order to process or reflect, they should have the freedom to seek a quiet corner or silent zone. Office design, in this case, is all about investing or reactivating some areas intended to reset and settle any internal agitation. Your office might have a designated meditation area, or the space might be conducive to meditation and breathing exercises done right at your desk.

Team members should have options for refreshing their minds and bodies quickly on a break. A Healthy Office will provide flexible options for its inhabitants to process in whatever way necessary so that whatever happens truly brings out the best in people.

Feedback

Finally, a creative way to encourage emotional control and expression is to design a method for open, written communication. A graffiti wall is a classic example. Team members are free to doodle and write creatively in such a way that their expression is visible to be appreciated by all. If your office design allows for it, this "creating wall" might become a permanent collaborative art fixture in the space. Alternatively, it might be something as simple as a communal whiteboard where creative engagement is encouraged but non-permanent.

Don't assume that a virtual office must forego creative, collaborative expression. The same technology that made working from home possible in the barest sense also enables programs like Mural, an online collaborative whiteboard. Even access to a team blog could fill this need for non-conventional expression within the workspace.

Further, any space feature that encourages written expression can also help people process information more effectively. Adam might be comfortable keeping all his considerations in his head, but Maya finds it beneficial to offload information onto whiteboards as it comes in. With all her work visible, she can work more efficiently and prevent herself from being overwhelmed before it is even a possibility.

Customisable office features are simple but effective in fostering community and expression, especially for those who tend to express their emotions visually rather than verbally.

Emotional diet is all about internal processing. The Healthy Office promotes a nourishing emotional diet by providing flexibility of expression and a sense of control, which overflow into each person's internal functions.

1.4: Spiritual Diet

Cultivating Spiritual Well-being and Organisational Purpose

Spiritual diet is the culmination of all three types of diets we have discussed so far. When I say that The Healthy Office promotes a vibrant spiritual diet, what I mean is that it has all the elements necessary to provide a comprehensive environment of purpose and well-being. Having conducted several studies on well-being in office settings, Beatriz Arantes defines well-being as "sustaining a healthy physical and mental state over time, in a supportive material and social environment." The Healthy Office promotes well-being by sustainably addressing all aspects of diet.

Imagine for a moment that you are a new hire entering your office for the first time. How does the office speak to you?

Is this a place that will live and breathe right alongside you?

Can you see your physical health only improve with time spent here?

Do you hear a whisper of inspiration and motivation?

Do peace and freshness of mind overwhelm you?

Are there clear options for both interaction and intense focus?

In other words, does the office herself introduce the ethos of your organisation to entrants? If the answer is no, then the solution is to first address each type of diet specifically. Once you have implemented some of those strategies from the previous chapters, then a few more considerations can start to pull everything together to promote a healthy spiritual diet.

To provide a world-class spiritual diet, an office will cultivate well-being on the backbone of organisational purpose. If everyone has one common purpose, it uplifts everyone by bringing them closer to the values and goals of the enterprise.

To achieve this through design, consider implementing visual elements that are closely associated with the company mission. You might incorporate the company colours or logos into the design. Informational displays might show real-time stats on the company and its achievements. Any bespoke design element that connects personal values to brand values can create a consistent sense of community.

Branding is not merely an outward-facing aspect of a company. The brand reminds people within the company that they are part of a unified, meaningful organisation. Arantes explains, "Without shared understanding of what you want to accomplish, it's hard to get people aligned on what their goals are and how to get there. People need meaning in order to know that their work is not going to waste." Many companies will verbally reinforce their vision and purpose to their team. When purpose is reinforced visually as well, however, the effect increases exponentially.

Again, although branding is more difficult to convey in a virtual environment, it is still possible. Consider providing your team with branded apparel or supplies. Even something as simple as a virtual Zoom background with your company's logo on it can do wonders for team unity and cohesion.

We have already discussed artistic installations that benefit emotional diet and visual satisfaction, but we can use these to promote spiritual diet as well by ensuring that they celebrate the diverse spiritual and cultural backgrounds represented in the office. Any type of inclusive design element elevates the sense of community in a place.

The most common advice for storytellers is "show, don't tell." The same principle applies here. You will never have to tell people what your organisational purpose is if you can show them through office design. If the well-being of your team members is evident from the moment anyone enters the space, you have already presented a persuasive argument for your company without speaking a single word.

This is the ultimate goal. You won't have to tell people that you work in a Healthy Office. It will be undeniable from the get-go.

Takeaways:

- The office can support nutritional diet by providing educational signage, healthy food options, and designated eating zones.

- Mental diet refers to a person's response to external stimuli. Workspace design should accommodate different personality types and work styles by including quiet zones for concentration, collaborative spaces for interaction, and biophilic elements to enhance well-being.

- The office environment should promote emotional regulation by allowing personalization and control over factors like lighting, temperature, and colour schemes.

- Spiritual diet essentially results from nutritional, mental, and emotional diets. The office can support individual well-being by implementing a comprehensive organisational purpose through design.

- The key to a healthy office is providing team members with options and the freedom to choose spaces that best suit their current needs.

Defining The Healthy Office: Diet

Attribute	The Status Quo Office	The Healthy Office
Nutritional Diet	Junk food or no food	Wholesome, healthy food options
Mental Diet	One type of space	Spaces for every need
Emotional Diet	Little opportunity for control or expression	Adjustable amenities and opportunities for creative expression
Spiritual Diet	Unclear organisational ethos	Comprehensive, ethical support for the individual

Explore how to implement healthy diet in your office by following the QR code below.

TheHealthyOffice.Com/Resources

2

Exercise

Energising the Workspace

Many people do not associate physical activity with the workplace, and understandably so. You might hit the gym after you get off work to relieve some shoulder tension from a long day at work, or maybe you make a habit of waking up to run or cycle before work. Either way, these things generally take place outside the office.

After all, how could people engage in physical activity at all during the workday? Why have we dedicated an entire chapter to exercise?

It's not rocket science.

Exercise leads to a better physical state. Someone who exercises regularly spends less time feeling low and more time on their game, so they are productive and healthy. Healthier team members are happier team members, and happier team members are role models in their ecosystem.

Essentially, when you can encourage one person at a time to be healthy through exercise, you can proliferate a healthy philosophy at your workplace.

Whether you promote healthy workspaces, develop them, evolve them, or only occupy them, start thinking intentionally about exercise.

2.1: Physical Movement Zones

Creating Active Spaces in the Workspace

"Sitting is the new smoking, you know." Maya had heard this phrase so many times, but for some reason, it struck her in a new way today. Her back ached from hours of sitting at her desk. She surveyed the office, noting how her coworkers either sat with painfully straight spines or with hunched shoulders, having given up on maintaining good posture.

When Maya visited her friend's office the other day, she couldn't quite believe what she saw. Team members frequently stood or walked around, not because they were going somewhere but just because they could. Standing desks were sprinkled among standard desks, but that wasn't all. A group of people seemed to be discussing a serious issue while pedalling an under-desk bicycle. Others lounged on ergonomic chairs while working on laptops or taking calls. The sheer variety of posture options was marvellous. Maya knew just by walking in that it was a Healthy Office.

Like Maya, we have all heard that sitting for extended periods of time has its dangers. But what is so bad about sitting, and is there a functional alternative?

The primary danger of sitting has nothing to do with the posture itself. The issue is that remaining in any one position for too long cuts off circulation. Circulation brings oxygen to your body, and if your brain is not receiving normal levels of oxygen, your thoughts start to slow down.

In order to maintain effective thought processes during the day, take a quick break every forty-five minutes or so to stand, stretch, and move around a bit, just to reboot your circulatory system. You are giving your brain a rest from focusing, reawakening your systems, and preventing a sedentary state.

Standing up once an hour seems like a small thing, barely even fit to be labelled "exercise." In truth, it is small. That is what makes it so effective. Anyone can take a few minutes to stand, shifting their position. And even that is a huge step toward The Healthy Office.

If standing breaks are only the first step toward implementing exercise in your office, then the good news is there are many more. Let's continue to define The Healthy Office through movement.

Standing desk areas are a different strategy to achieve the same results of discouraging sedentary tendencies and boosting circulation. There are many successful variations of standing desks, but all of them allow for team members to perform their regular functions while standing up rather than sitting. Ideally, these desks should be no different from normal desks except in height. Adjustable desks are even better because team members don't have to transfer any of their things to a new desk if they want to toggle between sitting and standing.

Our company, JTCPL Designs, has been part of several office journeys where we have been able to convey the benefits of adjustable standing desks and have gotten this implemented for 100 per cent of the occupants across facilities in excess of 100,000 square feet. These massive facilities will then have thousands of people using standing desks and boosting their health. Of course, this will only work for those open to redesigning their office or for those who are designing a new area.

On a smaller scale, you might consider investing in a designated number of standing desks that anyone can use when desired but that aren't dedicated to any particular person.

For smaller companies with an existing office, the best way to implement standing may be the forty-five-minute rule discussed above. Encourage team members to avoid static positions by standing for five minutes every forty-five minutes, and even while sitting or standing, shift positions every so often as well.

For those willing to invest more in multiple types of desks, there are many options that promote movement. Treadmill desk stations take standing desks to a new level, allowing team members to walk while they work. While this might sound distracting, walking at a very slow pace can boost alertness. For those with excess energy, walking can channel that energy for a more productive focus session. And as we have already seen, movement of any type promotes blood flow to the brain.

Cycling desks are another great option. You might be sitting at your desk while pedalling at any pace you like. These tend to work brilliantly for collaboration areas. Imagine a triangular setup of cycling desks, where an animated work discussion lends itself to the additional movement of pedalling. Sets of pedals could be built into certain desks, or you might have portable sets of pedals for anyone who wants to add them to their current desk setup.

Under-desk cycles and portable treadmills are entirely implementable for at-home workstations as well, so you don't have to miss out on that extra movement simply because your office is virtual.

Stretching does wonders for relieving tension during the work day. The best part about it is how scalable stretching is. Take a second to move your arms while in your office chair, or get up to stretch out your legs and back.

Take it up a notch and dedicate a corner of the office for stretching or relaxation exercises. You can include yoga mats, balance balls, and stretching guides for team members to utilise at their leisure. If you have a home office, reserve a space to keep a yoga mat or ball to use whenever you need to stretch out.

To go one step further, consider conducting yoga or tai chi classes for your team members. A full-body session is entirely possible within ten minutes, so a couple such sessions per workday is entirely reasonable. The physical benefit for the whole workforce will be immense.

If you have a large enough facility, you might consider including simple exercise equipment in mobility areas. Resistance bands can help with joint mobility while remaining undisruptive to office function. Hand weights also add another way to stay active. If this equipment is accessible and in line of sight, people will be visually stimulated and reminded to indulge in some form of movement. What you see always influences your subconscious thoughts, and you can easily help the office remain subconsciously focused on fitness.

2.2: Active Layouts and Circulation Paths

Promoting Movement Through Workspace Design

Physical amenities like equipment are extremely beneficial to cultivating The Healthy Office, but there are subtler design elements that can also transform your space and nudge inhabitants toward a more active lifestyle.

Consider for a moment the different departments in your company. Are there people who collaborate more often than others? Can you identify areas of heavy traffic between different parts of the office?

Efficiency norms might dictate that you place those two points as close as possible to prevent unnecessarily long walks, but what if you did the opposite? If places that experience high levels of collaboration are further from each other, you encourage those who make that walk to spend more time up and moving. The actual loss in time would be minimal, and the benefit to team members' physical well-being would more than compensate for it.

The other way to increase the necessity for walking during the workday is to place amenities strategically. Arrange the office so that water coolers, food stations, and break rooms require extra steps to reach. Again, this does not require significantly more time. It simply encourages regular movement.

In multi-level facilities, promote the use of stairs instead of elevators by creating staircases that are prominent, eye-catching, and attractive. Shifting between floors becomes a grand and appealing experience rather than a chore. If the stairs must remain utilitarian in design, consider giving the stairs playful graphics. For example, we have designed staircases that celebrate how many calories users have burned after climbing to each landing. While this is definitely not accurate, it motivates users into using the stairs more frequently than elevators. The graphics could also be gentle reminders about the virtues of an active lifestyle or other ways to stay active during the workday.

Finally, some meetings must be conducted while sitting around a table, and that fact might never change; however, if there are any meetings that don't require a table and visual displays, why not hold them while on the move? You can designate walking paths indoors or outdoors specifically for discussion purposes.

To add a bit of fun to your space, incorporate interactive floor markers such as marked walking circuits, hopscotch tiles, or footstep decals. Team members can engage in light physical activity by following the markers as they move through the space.

In one office, we designed a central ring corridor resembling a jogging track and even labelled it with distance markers to give it a sporty feel. Of course, it is much smaller than a full-sized track, but regardless, it serves the purpose of keeping people thinking about staying active, even if it's a subconscious thought.

In the locations where we have used some of these strategies, team members often engage in step-count challenges, which promote active movement as well as camaraderie and friendly competition.

If you are curious about how you might change up the layout of your office, explore online tools like CoDesigner, which allows you to virtually rearrange your office and test out these strategies.[7]

2.3: Fitness Facilities and Amenities

Integrating Exercise Opportunities into the Workspace

Some people have no problem spending a few extra hours of their day at the gym. But for most people, it's a lot of trouble to find the time to exercise between work, family, and other commitments. And time isn't the only problem. People also have to consider:

- Cost of a gym membership
- Transportation to and from the gym
- Instruction if needed
- Disruption to schedule

The good news is that the office can take care of certain obstacles so that team members can actively pursue their wellness with minimal difficulty.

Management often gifts their team members with small gifts like movie tickets or restaurant vouchers, but our offices tend to gift gym memberships instead. This is one tactic to eliminate cost.

If your office building has the requisite space, simplify the problem even further by building an on-site gym or fitness room. With full access to equipment, office inhabitants will enjoy the convenience of exercising before, during, or after work hours without the pain of additional travel.

If you can provide on-site facilities, remember to include showers and lockers to accommodate team members who engage in physical activity.

If you don't have the space for indoor gyms or workout rooms, perhaps you have outdoor space to utilise. Installing fitness equipment in green spaces or rooftops maximises available space and encourages people to enjoy fresh air while exercising. Outdoor spaces can easily be flexible as well. Transform the space for a group exercise class or martial arts training, then set up for an outdoor conference meeting later.

In large campuses, particularly those with thousands of team members, we include designated bike storage in our designs. If people want to move between their main office and a central cafeteria, they now have the option to bike there instead of walk, which is faster and encourages movement. Further, if people know that their office has designated storage and maintenance stations for bicycles, they may be more likely to cycle to and from their jobs.

Exercise is the perfect platform to fulfil the social quotient of your workspace. Host group exercise classes in your multipurpose spaces and bring in external experts. The benefit of bringing in experts is how well they can scale programs for your entire team. People will always have diverse levels of fitness, but if they can all participate together, you create a community that celebrates fitness. Those who are not as inclined toward exercise can be inspired to keep going as they see their peers perform movements that are still out of reach.

2.4: Ergonomic Workstations for Well-being

Designing for Comfort, Health, and Productivity

Ergonomics are essential to how The Healthy Office can support physical health. Proper ergonomic amenities enhance comfort and productivity and reduce the risk of work-related injuries and fatigue. There are plenty of ways to make your office more ergonomic, particularly if designing from scratch.

Dynamic seating options are essential for promoting movement and posture changes throughout the workday. Traditional static seating can lead to discomfort and health issues over time. Incorporating a variety of seating options can help mitigate these challenges.

Sit-stand stools are a versatile addition to any ergonomic workstation. These stools allow users to alternate between sitting and standing, encouraging movement and reducing the strain associated with prolonged sitting. By offering a higher seating position, sit-stand stools facilitate a downward tilt of the thighs, which helps position the lumbar region and pelvis neutrally. This positioning supports the spine's natural curvature, promoting better posture and mitigating the risk of back and neck pain. Additionally, the physical encouragement to get up and take breaks when feeling tired can help combat the negative effects of long periods of sedentary behaviour.

Kneeling chairs are designed to promote an open hip angle, which can help reduce lower back strain and improve posture. When you sit on a kneeling chair, the seat is angled at twenty to thirty degrees with a support pad at the front for your shins and knees. This position naturally creates the 'S' curve in your spine, helping to evenly distribute your body weight and take the weight off your lower back. By preventing slouching and engaging your core muscles, kneeling chairs can significantly improve your posture and overall comfort. They are also compact and economical, making them a practical choice for many office environments.[8]

Wobble stools encourage active sitting by allowing slight movements, which can help engage core muscles and improve balance. These stools have a curved base that allows for subtle rocking and rotating motions while seated. This constant, minimal movement helps fortify the core and back muscles, improving comfort and productivity. Wobble stools also enhance circulation, ensuring a better blood and oxygen supply to the brain, which promotes concentration and boosts productivity. Over time, active sitting on a wobble stool can develop an awareness of posture, effortlessly improving the way we sit or stand, leading to long-term benefits in comfort and health.[9]

While ergonomic seating is most common, there are other ways to introduce adjustable and supportive features to the workstation. Adjustable monitor arms allow users to position their screens at the optimal height and distance, reducing neck and eye strain. Monitors should be placed directly in front of the user, with the top no higher than eye level. This setup helps maintain a neutral neck position, preventing the discomfort of looking up or down at a screen for extended periods.

Adjustable keyboard trays enable users to position their keyboards and mice at a comfortable height and angle, minimising the risk of repetitive strain injuries. The keyboard and mouse should be close enough to prevent excessive reaching, which strains the shoulders and arms. Adjustable keyboard trays can significantly enhance typing comfort and reduce the risk of developing conditions like carpal tunnel syndrome by allowing for proper alignment of the wrists and forearms.

Footrests and anti-fatigue mats are essential for those who prefer sitting or use standing desks. These accessories can significantly enhance comfort and reduce fatigue. Footrests support the feet, helping maintain proper posture and reduce pressure on the lower back. They are particularly useful for individuals whose feet do not comfortably reach the floor when seated. By promoting a more ergonomic sitting position, footrests can help alleviate lower back pain and improve overall comfort.

Anti-fatigue mats are designed to reduce the discomfort associated with standing for long periods. Made from materials like polyurethane foam, they provide cushioning and support, helping to prevent fatigue and improve overall comfort. These mats encourage subtle movements that can enhance circulation and reduce the strain on the legs and feet, making standing workstations more comfortable and sustainable.

Proper lighting is another critical component of an ergonomic workstation. Ergonomic lighting solutions help reduce glare and eye strain, which are common issues in poorly lit work environments.

Task lighting, such as adjustable desk lamps, provides focused illumination for specific tasks like reading and writing. This helps control brightness and glare around monitors, reducing eye fatigue. Ergonomic desk lamps allow users to adjust the light colour from warm to cool and to direct light where it is needed most.

Air quality also affects the ergonomic comfort of team members. Ensure that the office is well-ventilated and free from pollutants. Use air purifiers if necessary to maintain clean air. As we have already discussed, certain plants act as natural air purifiers, filtering out toxins and chemicals. Good air quality can reduce the risk of respiratory issues and improve overall health and comfort.

2.5: Outdoor Work and Recreation Areas

Encouraging Activity and Connection to Nature

When Adam works remotely, he loves to sit outside and enjoy the fresh air. He can catch up on different tasks while feeding his mind and body through the nature around him, boosting his own creativity and productivity. He often wonders during these moments of tranquillity if there could be a way to enjoy the same peace during a day in the office. What if his building utilised outdoor spaces in such a way that it was easy for him to bring his work outside? Or how could he enjoy nature during his breaks without disrupting his day?

Incorporating outdoor work and recreation areas into office design can significantly enhance well-being in the workspace. These spaces provide a refreshing change of environment, promote physical activity, and foster social interactions among team members. And it only takes a simple change.

Rooftop gardens or terraces offer a unique and inspiring environment for team members to work outdoors. These spaces can be designed with comfortable seating and workspaces, allowing people to enjoy fresh air and natural light while working. Including outdoor charging stations can help with a seamless transition for your team. The presence of greenery can reduce stress, improve mood, and boost creativity. By providing a tranquil setting away from the traditional office environment, rooftop gardens or terraces can enhance focus and productivity. Additionally, these spaces can be used for informal meetings, brainstorming sessions, or simply as a place to relax and recharge during breaks. If you don't have outdoor space to utilise, consider transforming a room with greenery and plenty of natural light to simulate nature.

Another option for offices with limited outdoor space is to use balcony space. Standing desks are perfect for balconies because they require less space than traditional sitting desks. Working on a balcony provides the added benefits of fresh air and natural light, which can improve concentration and overall well-being. These spaces can also serve as a quiet retreat for focused work or as a spot for informal meetings and discussions.

Designing outdoor meeting areas with comfortable seating and shade can create an ideal setting for walking meetings or collaborative work sessions. Outdoor meeting spaces can inspire creativity and innovation by providing a change of scenery and a more relaxed atmosphere. Comfortable seating arrangements, such as lounge chairs or benches, can encourage open communication and idea sharing. Shade structures, like pergolas or umbrellas, can protect people from the sun and create a pleasant environment for extended discussions.

If you do have access to land, consider creating outdoor fitness trails with exercise stations. These trails can be designed for walking, jogging, or bodyweight exercises, offering a convenient and accessible way for team members to stay active. Regular physical activity has numerous benefits, including improved cardiovascular health, increased energy levels, and enhanced mental clarity. By incorporating fitness trails into the office environment, organisations can encourage a healthy lifestyle.

Courtyards equipped with recreational equipment like table tennis or basketball hoops can provide a fun and engaging way to unwind and socialise. These recreational areas offer opportunities for team members to take a break from work, engage in physical activity, and build camaraderie with colleagues. Playing games like table tennis or basketball can improve coordination, boost mood, and foster a sense of community within the workplace.

No matter what tactics you use to encourage fitness in your workspace, remember: movement is key. The Healthy Office is intentional about maintaining an active workday experience, even if the movements are small. Exercise promotes productivity, boosts "uptime," and supports the overall morale of The Healthy Office.

Takeaways:

- Regular exercise enhances physical and mental health, which leads to better productivity and a positive work culture.

- To create active workspaces, implement ergonomic, adjustable furniture and encourage frequent breaks to stand, stretch, and move.

- Design the office with movement in mind. Place high-traffic areas further apart to encourage walking and strategically position amenities to require extra steps.

- Providing on-site gyms or outdoor exercise equipment eliminates the extra effort required for team members to find and use a gym.

- Promote physical activity and social interactions through ergonomic and outdoor setups.

Defining the Healthy Office: Exercise

Attribute	The Status Quo Office	The Healthy Office
Workstations	Static	Dynamic and adjustable
Exercise facilities	Not applicable	Multiple options for gym access
Posture	No extra features	Ergonomic features

Explore case studies and turn your workspace into a wellness haven when you follow the QR code below or visit

TheHealthyOffice.Com/Resources

3

Sleep

The Foundation of a Productive Workspace

The rhythmic click-clack of keyboards mocked Adam's drooping eyelids. He'd been at it for hours, fueled by coffee and sheer willpower. His head bobbed, papers blurring into an indecipherable mess. Then, blissful darkness.

A gentle hand on his shoulder startled him awake. It was Maya, looking down with a surprisingly kind smile. "Adam, caught you napping on the job," she teased, but there was no judgment in her voice.

"Sorry, deadline crunch," he mumbled, sheepish.

"Actually," she said, "that's a sign you need a break. We have a new relaxation room downstairs. Why don't you take a power nap? Twenty minutes can do wonders."

Confused, Adam followed Maya. The room was dark, with plush armchairs bathed in soft blue light. Skeptical, he sank onto one. The cool air and gentle hum of a white noise machine lulled him back to sleep.

He awoke feeling refreshed, the room no longer a novelty but a haven. Back at his desk, the once-daunting report flowed from his pen. He glanced at the clock—twenty minutes exactly. Maybe a little sleep wasn't such a bad thing after all.

Like exercise, sleep is not often associated with the workplace. In fact, in most offices, you will get in trouble for sleeping while at work. But sleep is one of the most underrated and underdesigned aspects of the workplace. Think about it this way: the quality of your sleep is directly proportional to the length of your life. And when most of the workforce spends the majority of their lives at work, workspace design must address sleep. Sleep is a cornerstone of The Healthy Office.

I do not condone the practice of sleeping in the office in place of sleeping at home overnight. But The Healthy Office can promote quality resting habits for her team members while they are at work in many wholesome ways.

Sleep and Well-being

Sleep expert Matthew Walker has studied extensively the physical and mental benefits of sleep, as well as the results of sleep deprivation. Before we explore how The Healthy Office can support sleep habits, let me reiterate a few of Walker's findings.

Memory. Sleep renews the capacity to learn and retain new information. It both prepares the brain to intake new information and locks in that information after it is learned. Overall, sleep offers a twenty to thirty per cent boost to memory retention.

Emotion regulation. Lack of sleep has been linked to overreactive emotions. A sleep-deprived individual will experience more mood swings, with every emotion heightened to concerning levels.

Physical health. Proper sleep levels reduce the risk of heart issues, diabetes, excessive weight gain, reproductive issues, and immune system weakness.

DNA and lifespan. Insufficient sleep can alter the stability of genes and is associated with damaged DNA spirals. Healthy sleep schedules can prevent gene-associated diseases and extend lifespan.[10]

3.1: Quiet Zones for Power Naps

Designing Restful Spaces for Recharging

As Adam found out, quiet zones within the office can be a lifesaver for those who need a break from the constant noise and stimulation of the workplace. Just a short period of rest can leave team members rejuvenated and ready to be productive again. The size of the office does not matter when it comes to sleep. We designed a law firm's office, and its small team regularly worked long, stressful hours. We provided them a small room that could transform into a dark room, and team members regularly took full advantage of it to replenish their energy by taking power naps.

A designated nap area can be the first addition to your Healthy Office. These zones should be separate from the main work areas to provide a clear distinction between work and rest. By creating a dedicated space for short naps, team members can feel free to listen to their bodies' exhaustion cues and rest rather than feel condemned to push through brain fog and other side effects of sleep deprivation.

Within quiet zones, furniture should be comfortable and conducive to relaxation. You might include reclining chairs, nap pods, or daybeds that support a relaxed posture. These pieces of furniture should be ergonomically designed to provide maximum comfort and enable team members to rest comfortably. The goal is to create an inviting and restful environment that encourages the team to take advantage of the nap zones.

When you walk into a quiet zone, it should be immediately apparent that it is for resting. Soft, warm lighting can help reduce stress and signal to the body that it is time to relax. You can even create an entirely dark room with black-out curtains or shades to ensure absolutely no light enters.

Minimising external noise and distractions is critical for the effectiveness of quiet zones. Incorporate noise-cancelling features such as soundproofing materials, white noise machines, or noise-cancelling headphones. These tools help create a serene environment by blocking disruptive sounds from the surrounding office. Soundproofing materials can be used in walls, ceilings, and floors to reduce noise transmission, while white noise machines can mask background noise, creating a consistent and calming auditory environment.

Privacy is another key component of a successful quiet zone. The advancement of science has provided us with beautiful materials to use in these areas. Partitions, curtains, or frosted glass panels provide privacy and security during power naps. You might even consider acoustic partitions, which provide a buffer for noise and sightline. If you can only dedicate one room for resting, frosted glass panels offer a balance between privacy and openness, allowing light to filter through while maintaining a sense of seclusion.

Sleep pods are a fantastic investment as a replacement for nap rooms. Many different designs exist, but every sleep pod works to provide its single occupant comfort and isolation from their surroundings. They work toward recalibrating your circadian rhythm in the middle of a busy day. No one needs a full eight hours of sleep to feel refreshed during the workday. A five to twenty-minute dark room experience can do the trick. Sleep pods solve space issues as well because if you cannot dedicate an entire room to being a nap area, you can fit a few sleep pods in an office space and still achieve similar levels of darkness and quiet.

3.2: Sleep-Friendly Lighting

Supporting Natural Circadian Rhythms

We have discussed adjustable lighting as a general office feature, but let's get more specific. Circadian lighting is one of the best alternatives to natural light. It utilises LEDs aligned with the natural progression of sunlight throughout the day. The human circadian rhythm is the biological clock that runs a person's circulatory activity, emotions, hormones, and even eating schedule.[11] It is overwhelmingly controlled by the types of light a person internalises throughout the day. When artificial light disrupts contact with natural light, people tend to suffer from fatigue, poor sleep, moodiness, and reduced productivity. When your circadian rhythm is calibrated correctly, however, you can be more productive, creative, and healthier, all because your body can sleep at optimal times. By mimicking the sun's natural light, an office building can help residents maintain their circadian rhythms. These lighting systems adjust the intensity, colour temperature, and wavelength of light to promote alertness during the day and relaxation during the evening. By being in the office all day, inhabitants may experience better sleep at home and better focus throughout the day.

There are three main approaches to implementing circadian lighting systems: intensity tuning, colour tuning, and stimulus tuning. Intensity tuning adjusts the brightness of light fixtures throughout the day, while colour tuning changes the colour temperature to mimic the daytime-nighttime cycle. Stimulus tuning reduces blue light wavelengths during the evening hours to limit the impact on the circadian rhythm. These approaches can be used individually or in combination to create a more effective circadian lighting system.[12]

For time immemorial, the sun has guided the human sleep-wake cycle. With the introduction of artificial lighting, the natural cycle is often disrupted, making it difficult to sleep at night or wake up in the morning. For example, the sun does produce some blue light, but computer screens and phones produce much more. Blue light wavelengths tend to subdue the body's production of melatonin, a hormone that promotes and regulates sleep. In studies, participants who read on an electronic device before bed experienced fifty per cent melatonin suppression compared to those who read a printed book instead. Those exposed to blue light also had a decrease in quality of sleep, leading to an increase in exhaustion over the next few days.[13] To prevent these effects, reduce the amount of blue light that your eyes take in toward the end of the day.

There are several methods for blocking blue light, including special glasses and other physical blue light filters for screens. There are also software-based blue light filters you can install on electronic devices. The dynamic lighting systems available can help control blue light in overall lighting. It mimics natural daylight patterns, gradually changing in intensity and colour temperature throughout the day to align with the body's circadian rhythms.

Another way to manage lighting is to provide individual lighting options for different tasks. Adjustable desk lamps, for example, allow team members to customise their lighting environment, reducing the need for overhead lighting that can be too bright or harsh.

The most intuitive way to restore circadian rhythm for the whole office is to maximise natural light. If your office space has the potential for more windows, skylights, or light wells, utilise those as much as possible. If you are redesigning your office space, do so with natural light exposure in mind.

If you are working in a remote office setup, consider positioning your desk near a window so that natural light can regulate your body's sleep-wake cycle while you work.

Finally, regardless of whether you use natural light, circadian lighting systems, or normal lighting, you can always encourage your team members to reduce bright and overhead lighting in the workspace during the evening hours. This promotes a gradual transition to a more sleep-conducive environment as the day ends.

Chronotypes and The Healthy Office

A chronotype is the classification of a person's natural preferences for when to sleep and when to be most alert. Most people know their chronotype by the terms "early bird" or "night owl," but Dr. Michael Breus developed a more comprehensive classification system.

He identified four chronotypes, each determining the biological prime time for a person to sleep, get work done, and so much more.

<u>Four Chronotypes</u>

Lion. We tend to think of Lions as early birds. They wake early with high energy and high productivity. As a consequence of their early hours, they tend to go to sleep earlier as well.

Wolf. Wolves are more like night owls. They wake up late in the morning, but they also don't get tired until past midnight. They thrive in the evening hours when they are most creative and energetic.

Bear. Bears are in between. Over half of the population are bears, following a sleep schedule closely aligned with the sun. They might not wake up terribly early, but they can handle late hours if it's necessary. Bears do well with a typical 9-5 schedule.

Dolphin. Dolphins represent the smallest percentage of the population. They have an erratic genetic sleeping schedule. They tend to sleep lightly and struggle with insomnia.

When you know your biological chronotype, you can learn to optimise your sleep schedule and routine based on how you are genetically wired. Can this knowledge help you build a Healthy Office?

Yes!

If your team members are aware of their most productive times based on chronotype, they can plan important tasks for those times. They can also determine when rest periods or naps might benefit them most. For example, Bears and Lions would most benefit from an early afternoon nap, about 8 hours after they wake up. Dolphins and Wolves, on the other hand, should try to avoid naps to ensure that they can sleep well at night, but if they really need to nap, it should be later in the afternoon. The Healthy Office can provide her members with planned nap timeframes to maintain order and rhythm even amid the busy workday.[14]

3.3: Relaxation and Meditation Spaces

Designing Areas for Calm and Focus

Napping is an underrated tool for health. But it certainly is not for everyone. Especially if you have a Dolphin chronotype, sometimes the last thing you need during the workday is to invest effort in trying to sleep. Are there still restful design solutions for these team members? Of course.

This is where multipurpose rooms can shine. A study by Haworth shows a significant increase in lounge spaces as well as retreat spaces within offices throughout the world.[15] Because these secluded, casual rooms are already favoured, it only takes a small shift in mentality to deliberately use them for relaxation. A dedicated nap room is perfect for certain chronotypes, but sometimes, all you need is just a time of quiet to gather your thoughts. For that purpose, make sure your team knows that quiet rooms don't have to be used for napping only. They can be dedicated to meditation or relaxing as well. For some of your team, relaxation may look like reading a book or praying. The Healthy Office can provide physical and emotional space for people to relax and reset.

For most of the offices we design in the Middle East, a prayer room is an integral part of the setup. We have also designed several offices with multi-faith rooms to optimise space. If you are able to create a meditation room separate from the darkened nap room, then there are several extra design elements to consider. Comfortable seating is a given. For meditation purposes, consider floor cushions, meditation stools, or plush carpets. Ergonomic chairs and couches can also accommodate a variety of meditation and relaxation postures.

Ensure the decor of these rooms has calming elements. Paint the walls with soothing colours like muted blues and greens. Bright colours can be too stimulating to allow for proper rest. Soft, warm lighting also promotes mindfulness. Incorporate biophilic elements as well to gear your meditation room toward nature. A small water feature can evoke the feeling of a peaceful stream. Couple it with a few plants and wood-textured elements, and your team can have a nature-themed retreat from the hustle and bustle of the office. This is perfect for those city offices with very few natural elements outdoors. To help isolate this room from the rest of the office, make sure to use soundproofing materials and techniques.

Now that you've invested time and thought into creating an in-office haven for the team, don't let it go to waste. The busiest workers often find it difficult to take time to relax, especially in the middle of the day. They might try out the meditation room once or twice, but without proper direction, they won't be able to turn off their minds. To help, offer resources within the space, such as guided meditation recordings and meditation apps. When there is some guidance, people will be much more likely to follow through on their intentions to relax. You might even work with your peers to schedule mid-day meditation breaks, especially when you know the office will be dealing with high-stress situations.

Takeaways:

- The Healthy Office must incorporate quiet zones and/or nap areas within the workplace. These spaces allow people to take short breaks and power naps, which can increase productivity and reduce stress.

- Effective quiet zones should be separate from main work areas, equipped with comfortable furniture like reclining chairs or nap pods, and feature soft, warm lighting to create an inviting and restful environment.

- Circadian lighting mimics natural daylight patterns to support natural circadian rhythms. This can enhance productivity, creativity, and overall well-being by promoting better sleep and alertness.

- Recognising different chronotypes (e.g., Lions, Wolves, Bears, Dolphins) can help optimise work schedules and rest periods.

- Only some team members will benefit from naps, but anyone can utilise multi-purpose rooms for meditation, prayer, or quiet reflection. These activities provide a peaceful retreat within the office.

Defining the Healthy Office: Sleep

Attribute	The Status Quo Office	The Healthy Office
Energy Support	Exhaustion and sleep deprivation	Nap/rest periods built into the workday
Circadian Rhythm	Disruptive lights and schedules	Circadian or natural lighting
Environment	Arbitrary decor	Intentionally restful colours, lighting, and decor

Learn more about the unsung hero of workplace productivity when you scan the QR code below or visit

TheHealthyOffice.Com/Resources

4

Stress

Designing Stress-Resilient Spaces for Calm and Focus

Adam and Maya were known for their different responses to stress. The team even incorporated it into onboarding tips for new hires: "On high-intensity workdays, you might want to stay away from Adam!"

One hectic afternoon, Adam's frustration peaked. He found Maya and invited her for a coffee break with him.

"How do you do it? On days like this, everything is just too much. I can't breathe under all the stress, I can't sleep when I go home, and I snap at my coworkers even when they haven't done anything wrong. This is not sustainable, but I can't just stop caring!"

Maya smiled. "I know exactly what you mean. Look, believe it or not, I get stressed too. Almost all the time! But I learned to see stress differently. Stress itself isn't the enemy.

It's just the body's way of rising to a challenge. It's a signal that something important is happening."

"Okay," Adam said, "But how does that help?"

"Think of it like this," Maya explained. "When you're working out in the gym, you're putting physical stress on your body, right? When you lift heavier weights than normal or run a little further, that's like putting your body through a really stressful day of work. But you do it to train your muscles to deal with the stress, and gradually, what happens?"

Realisation swept across Adam's face. "You get stronger."

"Exactly. Mental and emotional stress can work the same way. When you don't let it get out of control, the stress is just a temporary discomfort that drives you to get stronger and more successful. I can give you some pointers on how to channel the stress."

> A stress-resilient workplace will prepare its inhabitants to be stress-resilient in every aspect of their lives.

Stress is the starting point for so many other issues. It can lead to mental illnesses and other health problems, and it can cause difficulty in relationships. Like Adam, many people take their work-related stress home to their families. Some try to solve the problem by sweeping their stress under the rug, but if people don't view their stress in the right light, they will never be able to utilise it positively.

To fulfil her purpose of well-being, The Healthy Office must address this stress crisis. The workplace should be an ecosystem that promotes positive stress responses. People tend to be a product of their environment. As the office is a frequent environment for many people, a stress-resilient workplace will prepare its inhabitants to be stress-resilient in every aspect of their lives.

What does it mean to be stress-resilient? When you are stressed, the first question you must ask is, "How am I going to respond?" If, like Adam, the stress makes you anxious, angry, and overwhelmed, then you have a non-resilient response. If, like Maya, the stress motivates you without controlling you, then you have a resilient response. Much of what determines your response is how you have prepared yourself before exposure to the stressor. Your office design can promote a proactive stress response in several ways.

4.1 Visual and Tactile Tranquillity

Design Elements to Induce Calm

Workspace design can play a critical role in overall stress management. An office crafted with stress resilience in mind can reduce the amount of stressful stimulation in one's environment. Stress will never go away. The only people who are truly never stressed are those who never breathe oxygen. However, work and relationships provide plenty of legitimate stress for one person. Any extra stress factors can be eliminated through intentional design.

We have discussed colour psychology as a strategy for nourishing emotional diet and for promoting a restful office environment. Choosing proper colours for your workspace will reduce stress as well. To reiterate, blues, greens, and soft greys are traditionally calming colours known to evoke tranquillity. Other palette options include anything earthy. Muted reds, rich browns, and other neutrals are grounding colours reminiscent of home or the natural world. You might choose a favourite landscape that evokes peace and choose your colour palette from that image. The goal is to create an environment that evokes memories of peaceful moments without distracting or engaging the mind.

As soon as colours are striking enough to draw attention on their own, they are no longer fit for the office. Anything too vibrant can cause disruptions to workflow or sensory overload, both of which either induce or exacerbate stress.

Your workspace can also encourage tranquillity through tactility. Materials affect the senses of both sight and touch, so it is important to use textures that reduce anxiety. Using elements like wood, stone, or greenery, you can infuse biophilic design into the workplace. The textures of these elements are reassuring to the senses, as they encourage thoughts of being outdoors or somewhere peaceful. They also add aesthetic value. People often underestimate the power of beauty to reduce stress. When people spend time outside, looking at nature scenes, or exposed to natural elements, they are predisposed toward a faster, healthier recovery from stress.[16]

Incorporate natural elements and materials whenever possible. For softer-textured furnishings such as rugs, curtains, and cushions, use calming colours and natural materials to aid in the calming effect. Including softer tactile elements can make a workspace feel comfortable and inviting, help absorb sound, and soften the overall mood.

It is difficult to imagine a workplace without technology. As such, digital devices are an important consideration when we speak of visual stress. Can staring at a screen all day cause unnecessary stress? As a matter of fact, it can. But the most stressful part of technology is the feeling that you might be missing out if you are not constantly checking notifications.[17] This pressure easily becomes another background stressor that affects your overall well-being without you noticing it. One solution is to establish tech-free areas to encourage disengagement from screens and work-related pressures. Sometimes, a short break is all it takes to disrupt that feeling of overconnectivity.

Also, be aware of how clutter becomes a visual stimulus. A workplace should be tidy, but an individual desk can easily build up material that fills your field of vision and causes unnecessary distractions.

In short, be intentional with the colours, textures, and sensory elements in your office. The Healthy Office presents an overall aesthetic that prevents extraneous stress response. When people do experience work-related stress, they will be able to look up, walk around, and be subconsciously calmed by their environment.

4.2 Auditory Awareness

Cultivating Stress-Resilience through Sound

I cannot emphasise enough the importance of acoustics for stress resilience. Noise is a potent stressor that triggers physiological and psychological stress responses in the body. It activates emotions like fear and anxiety, which triggers the release of stress hormones and leads to increased heart rate, blood pressure, and other physiological stress reactions. Chronic exposure to noise can contribute to the development of various stress-induced challenges with learning, memory, motivation, problem-solving, and aggression.[18]

Noise sensitivity varies among individuals, but even those with hearing impairment can experience heightened stress responses to sudden or loud noises. Even sounds that aren't themselves loud or disruptive can build up stress gradually in the listener's system. In a busy office, team members might not even notice that the ambient noises are stressing them out until they already feel the negative effects.

What is the solution? We cannot live or work in noise-less environments, and the absence of noise can be just as distracting. In our office designs, we rely on an acoustician to help us assess the quality of sound and address it as a design element rather than leaving it to default. But anyone can implement basic design solutions for sound in the workplace.

First, dedicate spaces with a lower decibel level. These can be your meditation rooms, your focus areas, your outdoor workspaces, or your relaxation zones. Use any space that can also benefit from noise reduction through high-quality soundproofing materials. Make the most of the spaces you have! Just ensure that your team members are aware of sound levels and they can escape to quieter environments on a regular basis. You can also utilise background music to relax your team and to serve as an audible reminder to monitor their noise-related stress level.

Consider installations that muffle sound to manage it in the larger, open-plan spaces. For example, soft furniture can absorb sound waves and reduce echo. Portable barriers designed to muffle noise can be rearranged to create private meeting areas in quick time with minimal effort. Acoustic panels take many forms, but there are types that can be installed on walls, ceilings, or desks. These will control extra noise, especially in those shared spaces.

4.3 Physical Peace

Preempting Stress Response through Ergonomics

We have discussed how ergonomic workstations support physical wellness, but we also need to consider how proper physical support systems can cultivate a resilient stress response. Proper back support prevents stress associated with physical discomfort.

Adjustable desks, ergonomic chairs, and lumbar supports help maintain proper spinal alignment and posture. Good posture reduces muscle strain and tension, combating physical stress before it can even arise.

When team members do experience back pain, it can easily compound any other stress they are under. When that happens, ergonomic furniture and accessories reduce pressure on the spine and surrounding muscles to alleviate the pain. Mobile workstations and adjustable furniture allow individuals to find comfortable working positions.

Increased comfort minimises and relieves physical stress from static postures, and muscle relaxation reduces associated mental stress. Include accessories like monitor stands, ergonomic mouse pads, and keyboard trays to support physical health and comfort. These ergonomic tools help prevent repetitive strain injuries and enhance overall comfort, reducing stress and fatigue.

One of the best ways to relieve stress is to do something active. Physical activity is one of the most effective ways to channel stress positively. Exercise releases endorphins that boost your mood while also burning off excess stress hormones. Physically, movement can release tension built up from remaining static all day. Mentally, being active takes your mind off any stressful thoughts and decisions. Even just ten to fifteen minutes of movement can make a big difference. So, ensure that your team has a place to stretch their mental and physical muscles. Provide a gym, allocate space for yoga and fitness classes, or design nature trails.

Alternatively, as we discussed in the exercise chapter, provide recreational sports and activities in the office. If you have the space for full sport courts, make sure they are accessible and fully stocked. If not, install table tennis or an area with board games in a corner of the office. Not everyone enjoys competitive activity, so you might also provide a well-stocked arts and crafts area. Take stock of what your peers would most enjoy as a stress reliever, and work with them to supply it.

By incorporating these design elements and strategies, you can create a workspace that enhances productivity and promotes the well-being and stress resilience of your team members. A well-designed, stress-resilient workspace fosters a positive work environment, leading to greater satisfaction and success.

Take Action:

The next time you sit down at your primary workstation, pause for a moment and do this sensory stressor assessment.

1. Close your eyes. Plug your ears, too, if it helps. Focus on only what you physically feel. What sort of chair are you sitting in? How does it support your body? What body parts are not getting any support? Are there areas, such as your neck, lower back, or arms, that are not touching anything but could be supported better? What about the feel of the desk? Are there tactile elements around you that bother you in any way?

2. Next, unplug your ears or focus on the sounds around you without opening your eyes. What noises do you regularly hear and tune out? If you work from home, do you hear your family in the background? Is your neighbour disrupting you? If you are in an office

building, how much of the ambient noise comes from your fellow team members? Based on their sounds, do you feel isolated or too close to them? Is there music playing?

3. Open your eyes and take in everything in your immediate field of vision. What impressions do you get? Are there busy patterns, loud colours, or distracting features? Is the space too empty or medical-feeling? Is your workspace cluttered? How does the overall aesthetic make you feel?

4. Finally, close your eyes again and focus only internally. What mental pressures affect you in the present moment? Are they work-related? Will they ruin the rest of your day if you do not immediately address them? Can you identify every pressure, or is there a looming anxiety whose source you can't pinpoint?

Now that you have distinguished between the sensory aspects of your workspace and your own mental stress, are there any changes you can make? Would a tidier work area cut down on the visual stress? Do you need to invest in noise-cancelling headphones? Or do the everyday sounds soothe you? A huge part of becoming stress-resilient is finding out what you need as an individual. What adds to your stress, and what takes it away? Ultimately, how can office design help you to relax?

4.4 Channelling Stress

Enabling Positive Stress Responses

Finally, how can The Healthy Office help her inhabitants channel stress when it is present? Are there strategies to ensure a positive overall effect? The most effective methods involve a personal mindset. While office design cannot directly change a person's perspective on stress, it can provide education and space for each person to make that choice independently.

The first step in channelling stress positively is to reframe how you view your body's stress response. When you're stressed, your heart rate increases, you breathe out of rhythm, and you may feel a surge of energy. Rather than seeing these as signs of anxiety, view them as your body preparing you to rise to a challenge.

People who view stress as enhancing rather than debilitating experience better health outcomes and performance under pressure. Tell yourself, "My racing heart is energising me for this task," or "My faster breathing is oxygenating my brain." This cognitive reconsideration can transform anxiety into helpful adrenaline.

One of stress's most powerful effects is sharpening your focus and attention. When you feel stressed about an important task or deadline, use that heightened alertness to your advantage. Try one of these strategies:

- Set clear, specific goals for what you want to accomplish

- Break large tasks into smaller, manageable steps

- Use time-blocking techniques to work in focused sprints

- Minimise distractions in your environment

You can harness that energy to get more done by directing your stress-induced focus toward productive tasks.

Sometimes, stress arises because something is important to us. Rather than trying to eliminate that stress entirely, use it as motivation to prepare and perform at your best.

For example, if you're stressed about an upcoming presentation, channel that energy into thorough preparation. If you're anxious about a difficult conversation, use that stress to carefully consider the other person's perspective.

Engaging in creative pursuits is another powerful way to transform stress into something positive. Artistic expression allows you to process difficult emotions while producing something meaningful. Ensure that every team member has access to notebooks for journaling or paper for art and doodling.

As you experiment with these methods for managing stress, develop a personal ritual or routine for whenever you start to feel stress taking over. A set process helps your brain shift gears and refocus your energy. You might find that one particular thing always reminds you that you are in control of your stress. Try one of these strategies:

- Take a prayer walk outside

- Listen to an upbeat song

- Spend 5-10 minutes in meditation

- Do a quick set of pushups or jumping jacks

- Make a cup of tea and savour it mindfully

- Recite a motivational mantra or affirmation

While we can't eliminate stress entirely, we can learn to work with it rather than against it. By reframing your stress response, finding positive outlets, and viewing challenges as opportunities for growth, you can transform stress from an enemy into a powerful ally.

Takeaways:

- Stress is unavoidable, but it does not need to be negative. A resilient stress response reframes stress as a positive force to encourage growth.

- Workspace design should minimise visual and tactile stressors, promoting a peaceful and productive workspace.

- Noise can be a significant stressor, so incorporating soundproofing materials, creating quiet zones, and using background music strategically can help manage auditory stress.

- Physical discomfort can exacerbate mental stress. Proper ergonomic design, including adjustable desks, ergonomic chairs, and lumbar support, is essential for reducing physical stress.

- To channel stress positively, encourage a mindset that views stress as an energising force. Set clear goals, break tasks into manageable steps, and minimise distractions to start using stress to your advantage.

Defining the Healthy Office: Stress

Attribute	The Status Quo Office	The Healthy Office
Stress Level	Stressful	Stress-resilient
Sensory Stimulation	Overstimulating	Non-distracting and comforting sensory elements
Stress Effect	Stress as inhibitor	Stress as motivation

Explore how office design can help you master your inner engineering by scanning the QR code below.

TheHealthyOffice.Com/Resources

5

Network

Fostering Connection and Growth

D o deep, lasting friendships—the "real" relationships—
always need to develop outside the workplace? Maya
had always wondered why everyone qualified people as
"work" friends versus just friends. She often found herself
acting differently at work than she did at home. Did her
coworkers do that too? Is that the reason she felt so estranged
from them when she ran into them outside of the office? She
wouldn't mind so much, except she really didn't have time to
cultivate friendships outside the office. She spent most of her
life with her coworkers, so why couldn't those count as real
relationships?

If you have ever been in the same situation as Maya, you
probably don't feel fulfilled. Human beings are social animals.
Whether you are an introvert, extrovert, or ambivert doesn't
matter. At their core, every person craves to be recognised

and grounded by a community, and the community that we spend about a third of our lives with is that work community. The Healthy Office seeks to remove the reservations between coworkers and create a lively, regenerative community among her inhabitants.

Collaboration is an underrated superpower in today's workspace. And I don't mean simply working together on a project. Collaboration in The Healthy Office means intentionally building bridges with your desk neighbours and those in the most distant departments. Authentic, dependable relationships ensure you produce your best work, feel good about yourself, and radiate positivity and gratitude wherever you go.

Community can often be the key that takes your business to the next level. It certainly was for Microsoft, for example. When Satya Nadella took over, Microsoft's stock price was thirty-seven-odd dollars. In only ten years, that price has increased well beyond tenfold. The secret, according to Harvard Business School's Professor Krishna Palepu, is how Nadella focused on culture. He emphasised the connections among his team, and that sense of community galvanised the whole company.

It will always be an individual choice to be vulnerable and authentic with coworkers, but there are office design strategies to naturally encourage that higher level of relationships. When the whole office is supportive and genuine, everyone involved will thrive.

5.1 Collaborative Work Areas

Designing Spaces That Enhance Collaboration and Teamwork

Imagine a workspace that sparks creativity and fosters collaboration at every turn. That's the power of well-designed collaborative areas. These spaces will encourage teamwork, ignite spontaneous interactions, and foster groundbreaking ideas.

Open-plan layouts allow your ideas to travel as freely as your colleagues. They are the secret ingredient to enhancing spontaneous interactions. By removing physical barriers, these spaces create an environment where team members can easily connect, share thoughts, and collaborate on projects. The result? A more dynamic and inclusive work atmosphere where innovation thrives.

Today's collaborative spaces can be as flexible as your team's thinking.

Where meeting rooms are necessary, they don't have to be one-size-fits-all. Today's collaborative spaces can be as flexible as your team's thinking. Imagine rooms equipped with modular furniture and cutting-edge technology that transform to suit any group size or meeting type. From intimate brainstorming sessions to large-scale workshops, these adaptable spaces can take collaboration from accessible to irresistible.

You can also dedicate areas to be catalysts for creativity. Most people are at their most creative when they can use visual tools. Provide picture zones specifically designed for idea sharing, complete with whiteboards, interactive screens, and comfortable seating. These aren't just spaces; they're incubators for innovation. Here, team members can gather spontaneously, brainstorm freely, and watch as their collective creativity gives birth to the next big idea.

Remember, a well-designed collaborative workspace is more than just a place to work—it's a tool that can dramatically enhance your team's ability to innovate, communicate, and create. By implementing these design strategies, you're transforming the way your team works together. Everything can change when your team is equipped with the freedom to interact spontaneously and genuinely.

5.2 Technology-Enhanced Spaces

Integrating Advanced Technology to Facilitate Connectivity

If you work from home or at a virtual office, you might be tempted to skip this chapter. After all, your Healthy Office has a population of one, and you collaborate with yourself every day. It might be time to rethink. Even if you don't see people face-to-face on a daily basis, you likely still work within a community, and there are foolproof ways to cultivate those connections.

Technological advancements have standardised video conferences even in traditional offices. More businesses are going global than ever before, and it's unsurprising when thousands of miles separate a functional, effective team. Regardless of your team's proximity, proper incorporation of advanced technology will foster connectivity and seamless communication.

High-speed connectivity is the lifeblood of today's workspaces. Internet bandwidth is more affordable than ever, so say goodbye to the days of laggy video calls and frustrating file uploads. With lightning-fast Wi-Fi coursing through your office and power outlets at every turn, your team becomes an unstoppable force of productivity. This isn't just about staying connected—it's about creating an environment where ideas can race at the speed of thought, and collaboration knows no bounds.

Virtual meeting facilities make collaboration ten times easier. State-of-the-art acoustics capture every vocal nuance. High video quality ensures clear communication through body language and facial expressions as well. Even using video messages instead of emails boosts your communication game. Communicating with audio and visual combined broadcasts passion and energy in a much bigger way than simply text. Virtual spaces redefine what it means to "be fully present." Remote team members aren't just avatars on a screen. The integration of virtual reality displays will take virtual meetings to a new level. Regardless of your team's location, communication can be seamless. Everyone can actively participate in a shared experience, fostering a sense of unity that transcends physical boundaries.

Other digital collaboration tools include interactive displays and digital whiteboards. These work for any type of office. Whether your team is huddled in the office or scattered across the globe, these tools ensure everyone is on the same wavelength. Sharing ideas and tracking project progress is easier when notes and diagrams are automatically digitalised and accessible to all.

5.3 Social Hubs

Promoting Informal Interactions and Social Bonding

Genuine bonding will never happen in a formal work setting if it cannot also flourish in an informal setting. To that end, consider how your office promotes interaction. Can you only find a seat when it's at your own desk? Does the arrangement of your seating areas imply confrontation? Is the leadership team ensconced behind a force field of glass?

Or do lounge areas beckon everyone in? Does the floor-plan invite you to meander down to your work area, greeting people as you go? If you get up to grab a coffee, does a cheer-ful conversation await you as well?

Expansive community tables and cosy lounge areas will cultivate ideas and friendships. These spaces invite your team to gather, share meals, and collaborate effortlessly. Here, casual conversations spark innovative ideas, and team bonds strengthen over shared lunches. It's in these spaces that your workplace transforms from a collection of individuals into a true community.

Remember the classic water cooler conversations? Now, imagine that energy multiplied. Strategically placed coffee and refreshment stations become magnetic hubs of interac-tion. Yes, they quench thirst, but they also quench the need for human connection. These spots encourage those chats that often lead to breakthrough ideas or simply brighten someone's day. When every team member is fueled by per-sonal interaction, they are automatically more secure and healthy.

Outdoor terraces and gardens are also perfect for cultivat-ing connections. These spaces offer a refreshing escape from the desk, inviting informal gatherings, open-air lunches, or moments of quiet reflection. Under the sky, your team can recharge, find inspiration, and return to work with renewed energy and fresh perspectives.

Social hubs are essential for promoting informal interac-tions and building a strong sense of community within the workplace. The Healthy Office becomes a vibrant ecosystem where collaboration and creativity thrive naturally.

5.4 Living Networks

Facilitating Personal and Professional Growth

The Healthy Office is fundamentally human-centric. The primary purpose of every design element should be to enhance the individual's journey through life. As every person benefits, the entire team will be propelled toward a company goal. When this happens, the workplace becomes a destination everyone looks forward to reaching. Strategically incorporating elements to foster personal and professional development and strong professional networks leads to a more engaged, innovative, and successful workforce.

To start, eliminate generic training rooms. Instead, equip small, quiet spaces with technology and resources to create "learning pods." These havens for focused learning support continuous professional development through online courses, self-paced training, or simply a distraction-free environment for reading and research. As a bonus, these learning pods can double as sleep pods to reduce cost and save space.

Invest in well-equipped multipurpose workshop rooms as well. Adaptable seating and audio-visual technology allow for interactive training sessions, workshops, and seminars. These dedicated spaces empower ongoing education and skill development, fostering a culture of learning that benefits both individuals and the organisation as a whole. Use these spaces for networking events as well. Equip them with flexible staging, lighting, and sound systems and host everything from casual get-togethers to informative talks and social gatherings. These allow the team to develop informal connections, but more importantly, they create a sense of belonging and community.

I have found that consistent celebration of individual achievements is crucial for fostering growth. At JTCPL Designs, we dedicate a day every month to celebrating the team. We collectively celebrate anything from birthdays of the month to player/s of the month and everything in between.

Imagine that you've been working diligently outside of work hours to write a book. It's finally done and published, and you share the news with a few coworkers. Would they celebrate with you? Would they spread the news throughout the office

Consistent celebration of individual achievements is crucial for fostering growth.

and hype you up? If the answer is no, you'll probably never work as hard for a similar achievement, or at least you won't tell your team members about it. The lacklustre effect will affect your work performance, too, as it reinforces the idea that your efforts are in vain. So celebrate any success with your peers. Create dedicated exhibition areas where team members can showcase their work, projects, and accomplishments. These serve as a platform for recognition, fostering a culture of appreciation and healthy competition.

Encourage curiosity between team members as well. Digital directories or interactive boards can showcase team members' skills, projects, and interests. This allows colleagues to discover potential collaborators and fosters connections based on shared expertise and interests, creating a valuable resource for building a strong internal network. Rotating desk assignments will nudge team members to connect with different colleagues. Similarly, incorporating team-based challenge areas—think brainstorming whiteboards or collaborative game zones—provides dedicated spaces for interaction and problem-solving across departments. These design elements help break down silos, promoting a more cohesive and innovative work environment.

By incorporating these spaces and design features, companies can create an office that fosters a vibrant culture of personal and professional growth. Plus, your Healthy Office will gain a reputation for promoting her individuals, and you will attract the right people when it comes to hiring.

Takeaways:

- A strong workplace community is crucial for team well-being, productivity, and overall satisfaction.

- Design strategies to encourage collaboration and teamwork include open-plan layouts, flexible meeting rooms, and dedicated creative spaces.

- Technology can enhance collaboration when leveraged properly. High-speed internet, virtual meeting facilities, and digital collaboration tools create a community no matter where team members are located.

- Informal interaction areas like lounges, community tables, and outdoor spaces foster social bonding and relationship building.

- The office needs spaces and initiatives that support individual and team development, such as learning pods, workshop rooms, and opportunities for recognition and networking.

Defining the Healthy Office: Network

Attribute	The Status Quo Office	The Healthy Office
Community	Only exists outside the office	Genuine work relationships
Technology	Fosters isolation	Fosters connectivity
Networking	Few growth opportunities	Self-improvement is celebrated

Continue your journey toward boosting personal and professional growth in the office when you follow the QR code below or visit

TheHealthyOffice.Com/Resources

6

Purpose

Incorporating Mission into Physical Design

Adam stepped into the newly redesigned office, his eyes widening as he took in the transformed space. In place of cubicles and fluorescent lighting stood an open, airy environment filled with natural light, living walls bursting with greenery, and a variety of workspaces designed to suit diverse needs and moods.

As he made his way to his adjustable standing desk, Adam noticed his colleague Maya emerging from a cosy meditation pod. She greeted him with a bright smile, her eyes sparkling with renewed energy.

"Good morning, Adam! Isn't this place incredible? I feel so much more focused and aligned with our company's vision now," Maya exclaimed.

Adam nodded in agreement. "It's like the office itself is breathing life into our purpose. I never thought a workspace could have such an impact on my well-being."

Throughout the day, Adam and Maya found themselves naturally gravitating towards different areas of the office. They brainstormed ideas in the vibrant collaboration zone, took rejuvenating breaks in the rooftop garden, and held a team meeting in a sunlit conference room adorned with inspiring artwork.

As the afternoon wore on, Adam noticed a palpable sense of unity among his coworkers. It was as if the thoughtfully designed environment had created an invisible thread connecting them all, fostering a shared vision and common purpose.

Later, while chatting over freshly brewed coffee in the office's cosy café area, Maya turned to Adam with a look of contentment. "You know, it's not just about the physical space. It's like this design has tapped into our collective consciousness, creating a shared dream for what we can achieve together."

Adam couldn't help but agree. The visionary office design had not only improved their physical health through ergonomic furniture and spaces for movement, but it had also nurtured their mental and emotional well-being. As they looked around at their colleagues collaborating, relaxing, and thriving in the various purposeful spaces, Adam and Maya felt a deep sense of gratitude for a workplace that truly understood the connection between environment, health, and shared purpose.

As the sun began to set, casting a warm glow through the floor-to-ceiling windows, Adam and Maya packed up for the day, feeling energised and inspired. They left the office not just as colleagues but as part of a community united by a common vision—one that their innovative workspace had helped to cultivate and strengthen.

We've discussed many individual aspects of workspace design that contribute to the creation of a Healthy Office. Subscribing to the mindset of each of the past chapters is essential, but the office must also be united by a common purpose. Imagine if Adam and Maya had access to stellar amenities, comfort, and support but no vision that bonded them to their company and each other. They might be happy enough, but neither would be entirely fulfilled by their daily work experience. People always want to be part of a greater cause. When the workplace can provide that common cause, you've set yourself up to create magic. I have seen it in all sorts of organisations: startups, mid-sized companies, and multi-billion dollar corporations. With the entire team aligned toward a single goal, everyone vibrates on the same frequency and shares a common dream, vision, and thought cloud.

Purpose feels like an abstract concept, but there are plenty of ways to make it tangible. As with anything, it starts with intention. Let's look at some strategies for incorporating vision into workspace design.

6.1 Mission-Centric Design

Incorporating the Organisation's Mission into the Physical Space

A shared sense of purpose within an organisation is essential for fostering engagement, loyalty, and productivity. One effective way to achieve this is by physically incorporating the organisation's mission into the workspace. A mission statement does not need to be spelt out to be effective. For example, everyone from my team at JTCPL Designs might not be able to articulate the vision of the company word for word, but they know without a doubt why we are there: we seek continual growth and improvement by creating an ecosystem of like-minded individuals; we are changing the language of workspace design and build through client-centricity and team-centricity; we enhance the lives we touch. Everyone in the office feels the strength of that purpose, and they are reminded of it daily through our designs. By creating and communicating a visual depiction of purpose, companies can continuously inspire and remind team members of their commonality.

Visual storytelling is a powerful tool for conveying the company's history, mission, and values in a memorable and engaging way. Here are some examples of visual storytelling in the office:

- Use customised art and murals to visually narrate the company's journey and milestones. For instance, a timeline mural in a central hallway can illustrate key events and achievements, making the company's history tangible and accessible to all.

- Incorporate brand elements such as logos, colours, and slogans throughout the workspace to reinforce the company's identity and mission.

- Display inspirational quotes and core values prominently around the office. These can serve as daily reminders of the company's mission and the principles that guide its operations.

Visual storytelling not only enhances comprehension and engagement but also facilitates cross-cultural communication, making the company's mission accessible to a diverse workforce.

We have also designed meeting rooms that are thematic to the ethos of the organisation. Themed meeting rooms can reflect various aspects of the company's goals or values, creating environments that inspire and motivate team members.

You might have an innovation room featuring current, cutting-edge design elements and the latest technology. This environment can stimulate creative thinking and problem-solving. Or, to emphasise the value of community, you might incorporate local art and comfortable, welcoming furnishings. This setup can foster a sense of belonging and collaboration among team members. A room dedicated to sustainability might use eco-friendly materials and showcase the company's environmental initiatives. You could create a similarly themed room for whichever company values are most important.

By designing meeting rooms that align with the company's values, organisations can create spaces that not only facilitate work but also inspire the team to embody the company's mission in their daily activities.

Strategic signage is another effective way to keep the company's mission and values front and centre. Motivational quotes work well in high-traffic areas such as entrances, break rooms, and hallways. You might also list core company values in thoughtful locations around the space. These signs can serve as constant reminders of the company's vision and goals.

Use directional signage to guide team members and visitors through the office while subtly reinforcing the company's brand and mission. For example, signs leading to the "Innovation Room" or "Community Room" can highlight the company's focus areas. You might also consider using interactive displays that allow people to engage with the company's mission and values. These can include touch-screens that showcase the company's history, achievements, and future goals.

Whether you use visual storytelling, themed meeting rooms, strategic signage, or all three strategies, you can transform your office into a space that physically reinforces the common goals of the team. This approach not only enhances engagement and satisfaction but also drives productivity and innovation, ultimately contributing to the organisation's long-term success.

6.2 Collaborative and Strategic Spaces

Facilitating Strategic Interactions and Decision-Making

In the African wilds, a watering hole is a place of peaceful congregation. Herds of diverse animals like zebras, lions, tigers, giraffes, and elephants all drink water together in harmony as the location fulfils a basic need for all of them. A central hub in an office building works the same way. Especially in large, multi-floor office buildings, it fulfils a basic need for your team to have a space where everyone can congregate to exchange thoughts and reinforce a sense of purpose for each other.

It might not always be necessary for the finance department to interact with engineering, but it is essential to provide a space where that can happen comfortably when it needs to. A central hub serves as the heart of the office, encouraging spontaneous and planned interactions that drive innovation and teamwork. And when every team in a large office knows their presence is welcomed and valued at the heart of the building, they support the company vision more readily.

Equip central hubs with comfortable seating arrangements that invite people to gather and engage in discussions. Consider using a mix of sofas, lounge chairs, and communal tables to accommodate various group sizes and activities. Provide collaborative tools such as whiteboards, sticky notes, and brainstorming kits to facilitate idea generation and problem-solving. These tools should be easily accessible and encourage hands-on participation. You can also ensure that central hubs are equipped with the necessary technology to support both in-person and remote collaboration. This includes high-speed internet, charging stations, and digital displays for presentations and video conferencing.

In one of our projects, a large European bank, we designed the cafeteria as a multipurpose central hub. Within thirty minutes, the team could realign the 200-seater cafeteria into a town hall arrangement. From there, the company could connect to their other offices around the world as leadership remotely addressed thousands of people at a time. Arrangements like this are extremely effective, and they demonstrate the necessity for advanced technology.

Integrating technology into collective spaces is crucial for supporting efficient and effective strategic planning. By equipping these spaces with state-of-the-art communication and presentation tools, companies can enhance productivity and connectivity. Interactive whiteboards allow team members to collaborate in real time, whether they are in the same room or working remotely. Video conferencing systems are becoming indispensable in supporting seamless communication with remote team members and external partners. This technology ensures that everyone can participate fully, regardless of their location. Other useful digital collaboration tools include project management software, shared document platforms, and virtual meeting apps. These tools streamline workflows and enable teams to work together more effectively. By integrating technology into collective spaces, companies can create an environment that supports continuous innovation and strategic alignment with the company's mission.

The European bank project demonstrates prime adaptability, which every hub could imitate. By implementing modular furniture and movable walls, companies can quickly transform spaces to meet the evolving needs of their teams. Particularly in large offices, bookable meeting rooms are notoriously difficult to secure at short notice. Movable walls enable anyone to create a meeting room in a few seconds, and a micro-team of four to six people could have a profitable brainstorming session in the central hub or another large space.

Adaptable workspaces enable companies to respond to changing demands and support a diverse range of activities, ensuring that the physical environment remains aligned with the company's mission and goals.

Any collective space is perfect for mission-oriented graphic design to feature. By investing in well-designed collective spaces, companies can enhance team member engagement, drive innovation, and ultimately achieve their mission.

6.3 Value-Driven Environments

Reflecting and Promoting Organisational Values

In most of our projects, we place an enormous emphasis on sustainability. Generally, these supremely sustainable offices are certified as LEED platinum-rated by the U.S. Green Building Council (USGBC). LEED stands for Leadership in Energy and Environmental Design. It is a globally recognised certification system developed by the USGBC to promote sustainable and environmentally friendly building practices. In workspace design, LEED certification signifies that a building or space has been designed and built using strategies aimed at improving performance across several key areas. Sustainability is important, but even more important is the sense of satisfaction that team members have knowing they work in a "green environment." To that end, we use environmental graphic design to ensure people know they are walking in a Platinum LEED Certified facility.

In some cases, LEED certification may not be feasible for several reasons. When this is the case, simple sustainable practices include using renewable materials, energy-efficient systems, and green spaces to reflect the company's commitment to environmental stewardship. Incorporating natural light, plants, and eco-friendly materials can also enhance well-being and productivity.

These are only some examples of how you might tailor the workplace environment to reflect and promote the organisation's values. Innovation labs are another method. These could be spaces dedicated to experimentation, where team members can go to test new ideas and technologies. Inside these labs, provide access to state-of-the-art tools and resources such as 3D printers, virtual reality setups, or advanced computing systems. The lab's aesthetic should inspire creativity, which might involve vibrant colours, unconventional furniture, or inspirational art displays.

You can conduct workshops in the lab or conduct product development, but regardless of what you use it for, make sure that this is a space where leadership can converge with team members, especially newer ones. The more leaders speak with newcomers, the more quickly the ethos of the organisation is proliferated, and an innovation lab is a great place to foster such discussion.

Innovation labs serve as a physical manifestation of a company's commitment to progress, creativity, and learning. They provide a safe space for experimentation and failure, crucial elements in the innovation process. Learning is extraordinarily effective at bringing people together in a conducive environment. People come on equal footing and collectively grow in understanding. Having a space designed specifically for learning and development can do wonders for furthering the company's ethos.

Finally, consider opening up space in your office to the greater community. Create spaces that can be used by local community groups or for company outreach programmes. This not only underscores a commitment to community involvement but also provides opportunities for team members to engage in meaningful activities outside their regular work. When companies create valuable connections with their local area, they enhance their reputation and reinforce their commitment to wholesome and uplifting values.

6.4 Engaging and Motivational Settings

Immersing Team Members in the Organisation's Cultural Ethos

Crafting spaces that motivate and engage team members by immersing them in the organisation's cultural ethos is key to maintaining a vibrant workplace culture. By strategically incorporating cultural artefacts, interactive displays, and recognition areas, companies can create an environment that reflects their values and fosters a sense of belonging and pride.

Cultural artefacts are tangible items that hold significant meaning within the organisation, symbolising its history, achievements, and values. Displaying these artefacts prominently in the workplace can serve as a constant reminder of the company's legacy and aspirations.

Displaying awards, patents, and other recognitions can highlight the company's accomplishments and inspire pride among team members. These items serve as a testament to the hard work and dedication of the team. Showcasing historical items such as products, prototypes, or memorabilia that represent significant milestones in the company's journey can provide a sense of continuity and connection to the past. Items that are unique to the company's industry, such as specialised tools or equipment, can reinforce the organisation's identity and expertise.

Interactive displays are dynamic tools that can engage team members by providing real-time information and fostering collaboration. These digital interfaces can be used to share company news, updates, and achievements, creating a lively and informative environment.

Consider creating a recognition area as a dedicated space within the office where team successes and individual achievements are celebrated. These areas can help foster a culture of appreciation and motivation, encouraging everyone to strive for excellence.

Recognition walls might celebrate temporary achievements like "Team Member of the Month" or "Project Rock Stars," and posting project milestones can provide visible acknowledgement of hard work and dedication. Showcasing trophies, plaques, and other awards in a prominent location can serve as a constant reminder of the company's successes and the contributions of its team members. Digital displays can highlight top performers, project achievements, and other recognitions, creating a sense of healthy competition and motivating teams to excel.

By thoughtfully designing these spaces, organisations can foster a sense of pride, belonging, and motivation among their team members. This approach not only strengthens the cultural foundation of the company but also drives engagement, satisfaction, and productivity, ultimately contributing to the organisation's long-term success.

6.5 Reflective and Thoughtful Design

Reflecting on the Company's Past Achievements and Future Aspirations

One of the more striking walls we have helped design was at the office of a legacy company. They had been in business for fifty-plus years, and we decided to create a history wall for them, detailing the entire story of the organisation. It stands in the public interface area, where visitor frequency is highest, and everyone can see and appreciate it. For visitors, it visually establishes the reputation and dependability of the company, and for owners, promoters, and team members, it promotes gratefulness for the journey they have travelled to be here.

Heritage corners work the same way. These areas showcase the company's history and evolution, offering team members a sense of legacy and continuity. You might include historical photographs, artefacts, and stories that highlight key moments in the company's journey. Just as heritage areas look back in time, a visionary space looks forward, showcasing the possibilities of the future. They can be equipped with inspiring views or calming elements to promote reflection, or they could depict the visionary goals of the company. These areas can provide a serene environment for team members to think about the future and develop innovative ideas.

Any of these design elements might be exactly what your office needs to encourage a visionary perspective for all her inhabitants. Purpose is the essence of The Healthy Office. When you are purpose-driven, you have a sense of optimism that puts a spring in your step. You look to the future with hope and determination, and that mentality, above all others, will truly transform your workspace.

Takeaways:

- A strong company vision and shared goals are essential for creating a truly fulfilling work environment.

- When physical spaces align with a company's purpose and values, it creates a more meaningful and inspiring work experience. Sustainable design features, innovation labs, and community spaces physically embody and reinforce a company's commitment to principles like environmental stewardship, creativity, and community engagement.

- Central hubs facilitate diverse interactions, foster innovation, and reinforce the company's vision. Adaptable designs support various activities and strengthen team alignment with organisational goals.

- To foster a sense of belonging, pride, and motivation among team members, The Healthy Office can utilise cultural artefacts, interactive displays, and recognition areas.

- History walls, heritage corners, and visionary spaces celebrate a company's past achievements and future aspirations, fostering a sense of legacy, continuity, and purpose among team members and visitors.

Defining the Healthy Office: Purpose

Attribute	The Status Quo Office	The Healthy Office
Mission Statement	Unclear, unintegrated	Integrated into office design
Values	Unemphasized	Reflected in the environment
History and Vision	Unknown	Depicted in physical displays

Explore the possibilities of North Star guidance in
The Healthy Office by following the
QR code below or visit

TheHealthyOffice.Com/Resources

7

Your Healthy Office

ongratulations! By completing this book, you've taken the first step toward democratising well-being in the workplace. By exploring what The Healthy Office looks like, you have already displayed remarkable investment in yourself and your team.

It's been said that with great power comes great responsibility. The strategies presented here give you the power. Now, you have the opportunity to take responsibility for the people and offices in your proximity. What does that look like? Let me offer you a few actionable plans:

- Personally commit to The Healthy Office and encourage your team to do so as well. Many of the strategies I've discussed begin with an intentional mindset. Remember that we began this journey with the FCD philosophy. As you begin to implement small changes to your office space, remember to do so with Focus, Consistency, and Discipline. Above all, value people as the most precious resource of all.

- Study the book with your team and formulate an action plan. Some of the interventions presented in this book can be implemented simply, but others require more forethought. Spend time with your team strategising the most effective ways to create a Healthy Office for yourselves. You will have to prioritise based on your company's values and resources, but above all, do your best to address every aspect of The Healthy Office. The acronym DESIGN will help you remember:

  - **D**iet: nutritional, mental, emotional, and spiritual
  - **E**xercise: movement and physical support
  - **S**leep: restful environments
  - **I**nner-Engineering: stress resilience
  - **G**rowth: success networks
  - **N**orth Star: purpose and direction

- If you want expertise in creating or redesigning your office, JTCPL Designs invites you to start your Healthy Office journey with a discovery call. We have designed millions of square feet of offices through hundreds of projects over more than two decades. We would be very happy to come alongside you as a co-passenger on your own journey. Reach out to us at TheHealthyOffice.com or explore our work at JTCPLDesigns.com.

The Healthy Office is attainable for anyone, anywhere. The office of your dreams is within reach. It is up to you to make it your reality!

Complete Healthy Office Chart

Attribute	The Status Quo Office	The Healthy Office
Objective	Profit	Happiness
Duration	Temporary	Timeless
Solutions	Low-level physical changes	High-level strategies
Nutritional Diet	Junk food or no food	Wholesome, healthy food options
Mental Diet	One type of space	Spaces for every need
Emotional Diet	Little opportunity for control or expression	Adjustable amenities and opportunities for creative expression
Spiritual Diet	Unclear organisational ethos	Comprehensive, ethical support for the individual
Workstations	Static	Dynamic and adjustable
Exercise facilities	Not applicable	Multiple options for gym access
Posture	No extra features	Ergonomic features
Energy Support	Exhaustion and sleep deprivation	Nap/rest periods built into the workday
Circadian Rhythm	Disruptive lights and schedules	Circadian or natural lighting
Environment	Arbitrary decor	Intentionally restful colours, lighting, and decor
Stress Level	Stressful	Stress-resilient
Sensory Stimulation	Overstimulating	Non-distracting and comforting sensory elements
Stress Effect	Stress as inhibitor	Stress as motivation
Community	Only exists outside the office	Genuine work relationships
Technology	Fosters isolation	Fosters connectivity
Networking	Few growth opportunities	Self-improvement is celebrated
Mission Statement	Unclear, unintegrated	Integrated into office design
Values	Unemphasized	Reflected in the environment
History and Vision	Unknown	Depicted in physical displays

Endnotes

1   Shawn Achor, https://www.steelcase.
    com/research/articles/topics/wellbeing/
    wellbeing-a-bottom-line-issue/
2   https://www.mmoser.com/ideas/
    workplace-neurodiversity/
3   *Ideation Exploration*, Haworth, May 2024
4   Nieuwenhuis et. al. "The Relative Benefits of Green
    Versus Lean Office Space: Three Field Experiments,"
    2014, https://gwern.net/doc/psychology/
    nature/2014-nieuwenhuis.pdf, Accessed 6 Aug. 2024.
5   https://www.workdesign.com/2012/07/
    the-benefits-of-plants-in-the-workplace/
6   Beatriz Arantes, https://www.steelcase.
    com/research/articles/topics/wellbeing/
    wellbeing-a-bottom-line-issue/

7   https://www.haworth.com/eu/en/services/consultancy/codesigner.html

8   Bettany-Saltikov, J., Warren, J., & Jobson, M. "Ergonomically designed kneeling chairs are they worth it?: Comparison of sagittal lumbar curvature in two different seating postures. *Studies in Health Technology and Informatics*, 140, 103–106, 2008. Accessed 6 Aug. 2024.

9   Doroff, Claire E et al. "Effects of Active Sitting on Reading and Typing Task Productivity." *International Journal of Exercise Science* vol. 12, pp. 1216-1224. 1 Nov. 2019. Accessed 6 Aug. 2024

10 Walker, Matthew. *Why We Sleep: Unlocking the Power of Sleep and Dreams.* Scribner, 2017.

11 Walker, Matthew. *Why We Sleep: Unlocking the Power of Sleep and Dreams.* Scribner, 2017.

12 https://www.thelightingpractice.com/what-is-circadian-lighting/

13 Walker, Matthew. *Why We Sleep: Unlocking the Power of Sleep and Dreams.* Scribner, 2017.

14 Breus, Michael. *The Power of When: Discover Your Chronotype–and Learn the Best Time to Eat Lunch, Ask for a Raise, Have Sex, Write a Novel, Take your Meds, and More.* Mindworks, Inc. 2016.

15 *Ideation Exploration*, Haworth, May 2024

16 Brown, Daniel K, et al. "Viewing Nature Scenes Positively Affects Recovery of Autonomic Function Following Acute-Mental Stress," https://www.ncbi.nlm.nih.gov/pmc/articles/PMC3699874/. Accessed 6 Aug. 2024.

17 "Stress in America: Coping with Change, Part 2: Technology and Social Media," American Psychological Association, https://www.apa.org/news/press/releases/

stress/2017/technology-social-media.pdf. Accessed 6 Aug. 2024.

18 Westman, Jack C., and James R. Walters. "Noise and Stress: A Comprehensive Approach." https://www. ncbi.nlm.nih.gov/pmc/articles/PMC1568850/pdf/ envhper00468-0281.pdf. Accessed 6 Aug. 2024.

Acknowledgements

Shri Swami Samartha

First and foremost, this book is a tribute to Aai and Baba, whose blessings have made me who I am.

My heart and soul mate Poonam, nothing would have been possible without you. Rhea and Ruchi, the best daughters one could have, you inspire me to bring out my best.

My sister, Rachana, my first fan and follower. You have inspired me in more ways than you can imagine.

Vipul, my main man, who chose to embark on this journey when it was only a dream, I am grateful beyond words. Jairam and Siddharth, your support has made a miraculous difference. Aniket, your relentless efforts always inspire me.

Suzanne and Zulfi, your friendship makes me a better person.

Pierre, I am so grateful to know you are beside me.

Acknowledgements

My business partner, Nitin, you are the kindest soul I know.

My guide and mentor, Dan Sullivan, who keeps inspiring me with his own example; Babs Smith, who is a reference point to me; I am deeply grateful and consider myself fortunate to have you in my Life.

My mastermind family, Iman Mutlaq, Chad Willardson, and Dr. Ehab Hamarneh, who keep nudging me for success.

Drs. Marcia Griffin-Hansraj and Ken Hansraj, my family in the United States.

Entrepreneurs Organization–Mumbai, more specifically, my forum of ten years and counting, Toral, Rosenyn, Tanveer, Dinesh, Ankur, Achal, Ashish, and Bobby.

To my JTCPL Designs family, whose support has created magic through the years, I am beyond grateful. All our clients whose offices we have worked on have provided me with unprecedented insights into the realm of workspace design.

Ninad Gupte, whose expertise helped me acquire the domain TheHealthyOffice.com

Megha Awasthy and Praveen Rawal, who have been bouncing boards right from the start of this book. I am beyond grateful for your wisdom.

Tracy Brower and Gale Moutrey from M/s Steelcase, our conversations always reminded me of a better future.

Henning Figge and Stefan Kiss from M/s Haworth, your encouragement was a great support.

My nutrition coach, Kinita, our journey has been stellar and fun-filled! Thank you for your wisdom!!

My fitness coach and dear friend, Nupur Shikhare, you are simply amazing! Look where we have reached!!

Mikaeel Memon, our conversation sowed the seed for The Healthy Office. Thank you!!

Ninette Kohler, your valuable insights at the perfect time enhanced the message.

To my publishers, Igniting Souls, Kary Oberbrunner, Sarah Grandstaff, Ruthie Bult, Elizabeth Haller, Jill Ellis, Melissa Fultz, Tanisha Williams, David Samuel, and Heather Parady. You are totally amazing!

To all my connections and followers on the digital realm, thank you for the support over the years.

About the Author

Ninad Tipnis is an award-winning architect, author, and the Founder and Principal of JTCPL Designs, with over two decades of experience. Recognised with several prestigious awards, including the Institute of Indian Interior Designers Award, IndeXellence Award, Society Interiors Award for outstanding contribution to commercial design, and Architects & Interiors India's Hot 100, Ninad's work stands out in the industry.

Born into a family of distinguished architects, Ninad's passion for architecture was evident from an early age. He pursued his passion at the Academy of Architecture, where he realised that quality architecture is about more than aesthetics and honed his creative flair for creating spaces that inspire happiness and success.

Ninad's designs are known for their vibrant colours and range from minimalist to richly ornate, creating environments that foster efficiency, collaboration, and innovation. At JTCPL Designs, these values are upheld in projects across the globe.

Ninad's expertise extends beyond architecture. He delves into understanding human psychology, motivation, health, and the impact of spaces on people's lives. Passionate about learning, human longevity, peak performance, and human potential, Ninad is a lifelong student who continuously expands his knowledge in these areas.

He is an avid reader, a fitness enthusiast who has completed several marathons, and a member of the Entrepreneurs' Organisation (EO) in the Mumbai and Dubai chapters. Ninad currently resides in Dubai with his wife, where he continues to inspire through his work and philosophy.

Connect with Ninad at TheHealthyOffice.com.

CONNECT WITH NINAD

Follow him on your favorite social media platforms today.

Ninad Tipnis

ninadtipnis

JTCPLDesigns.com

CONNECT WITH

Follow them on your favorite
social media platforms today.

JTCPL Designs

jtcpl_designs

JTCPLDesigns.com

HEALTHY OFFICE TRACKER

HOW **HOT** IS YOUR OFFICE?

TheHealthyOffice.com/Resources

Printed in the USA
CPSIA information can be obtained
at www.ICGtesting.com
LVHW010052220924
791582LV00007B/16/J

9 781636 802725